Published by Southwest Specialty Food, Inc.
5805 West McLellan
Glendale AZ 85301
1-800-536-3131
www.asskickin.com
© 1997 Southwest Specialty Food, Inc.
Printed in U.S.A.
First edition

Library of Congress Cataloging-in-Publication Data

Southwest Specialty Food, Inc.
Ass Kickin'™ Cookbook

Includes index.
1. Cookery, Hot & Spicy. 2. Spices.
3. Condiments. I. Title.
ISBN 0-9647529-0-5

INTRODUCTION

The first Ass Kickin'™ cookbook was written especially for those who love tongue torching, tonsil sizzling, south of the border hot dishes. Any meal, special event, or party is more exciting and enjoyable when unique snacks, drinks, and meals are served. So now, with this Ass Kickin'™ cookbook, you can become the most envied host or hostess in your neighborhood.

For starters, try the Ass Kickin'™ Chicken Tamale Pie or the Ass Kickin'™ Barbecued Brisket - two of our favorites. And just two of over 180 HOT gourmet recipes you'll find tucked inside this Ass Kickin'™ cookbook!

Southwest Specialty Food, Inc., the world's largest habañero specialty food manufacturer, is proud to provide you, our all-important customer, with plenty of tantalizing hot dishes fit for a king. So read on, and discover for yourself, just how easy it is to prepare all those HOT dishes you've been dreaming about.

And remember - you're the chef - so please enjoy substituting our Ass Kickin'™ products whenever you feel the urge. These are great recipes whether you make them Ass Kickin'™ hot or not.
Please feel free calling us at 1-800-536-3131 or visit our web site at www.asskickin.com to find a location nearest you for all the Ass Kickin'™ supplies your kitchen and gourmet cook can handle.

ASS KICKIN' CONTENTS

BEVERAGES

BLOODY MARY

INGREDIENTS:

• 1 (12 oz.) can tomato juice or V-8

• 2 oz. gin or vodka

• Season with salt and pepper, to taste

• 2 to 4 dashes of tabasco, or for an Ass Kickin'™
  Bloody Mary, add two dashes Ass Kickin'™ Cajun
  Hot Sauce

• Dash of worcestershire sauce

• Lemon wedges

• Celery stalks

• Ice

DIRECTIONS:

Combine first five ingredients. Pour over ice into
tall glasses. Add celery stalk and lemon wedge. Serves 2.

6

FROZEN DAIQUIRIS

INGREDIENTS:

- 1 (16 oz) can frozen limeade concentrate (undiluted)

- 3 cans water (use limeade concentrate can)

- 2 to 3 cans light rum (using limeade can to measure)

DIRECTIONS:

In a medium size freezer safe bowl, combine all 3 ingredients and freeze. The mixture will not freeze solid due to the rum.   Before serving, place half of the mixture in a blender and blend only until slushy consistency. Pour into cocktail glasses.   Serve with a short straw.

Variations; add to blender at time of mixing; 1/2 cup strawberries; pineapple or raspberries.

HOT BUTTERED RUM

INGREDIENTS:

- 1 lb. light brown sugar

- 1 lb. butter, room temperature

- 1 quart vanilla ice cream (quality brand)

- Rum; either dry white or spiced

DIRECTIONS:

Combine brown sugar and butter in a large mixing bowl; beat until blended and smooth. Add ice cream ; beat until blended well. Store in a covered container in the freezer. Remove when ready to serve.   For each serving ; place 1 heaping tbsp. batter to coffee mug, fill cup with hot water and add as much rum as desired. Stir until batter is melted, and serve hot. Batter will store in freezer for several months.

8

ASS KICKIN'

KAHLUA

INGREDIENTS:

- **4 cups water**

- **3 3/4 cups sugar**

- **2 oz. instant coffee granules**

- **1 quart vodka**

- **1 vanilla bean, split**

DIRECTIONS:

Bring water to boil, add sugar and continue boiling for 5 minutes. Remove from heat and add instant coffee. Cool for 5 to 10 minutes. Add vodka and mix. Split vanilla bean and place in 1/2 gallon sealable jar, pour in Kahlua mixture. Seal jar and allow to stand for 2 to 4 weeks.

KAHLUA COFFEE

INGREDIENTS:

• 1 oz. Kahlua

• 1 tsp. chocolate syrup

• Dash of cinnamon

• Hot coffee

• Sweetened whipped cream

DIRECTIONS:

Place Kahlua, chocolate syrup, cinnamon, and hot coffee in
cup or mug. Stir to blend. Top with whipped cream.
Serves 1.

MARGARITAS

INGREDIENTS:

- 8 oz. tequila

- 3 oz. Triple Sec

- 4 tbsp. lime juice

- Ice cubes

- Lime wedge

- Coarse salt

- Add a few dashes Ass Kickin'™ Hot Sauce for a little zing in your margarita

DIRECTIONS:

Combine tequila, Triple Sec, lime juice, Ass Kickin' Hot Sauce™ and ice in blender. Blend until smooth. Rub lip of glasses with lime wedge and dip in salt to coat. Fill glasses. Serves 4.

11

MARTINI

INGREDIENTS:

• 2 oz gin or vodka (best if you use high quality)

• 1 to 2 splashes dry vermouth

• Ice cubes

• 1 pickled habanero

DIRECTIONS:

Place gin or vodka, vermouth and ice cubes in a cocktail shaker. Shake until well chilled. Strain into a conventional martini glass or in a larger glass for one on the rocks. Garnish with a habanero pepper.

ASS KICKIN'™

MEXICAN EGG NOG

INGREDIENTS:

- 2 cups milk

- 2 cups half-and -half

- 1 1/2 tsp. vanilla

- 1/2 cup sugar

- 8 egg yolks

- 1/4 to 1/2 cup light or dark rum

- Cinnamon sticks (enough for all servings)

DIRECTIONS:

In a 3-quart sauce pan, bring milk and half-and -half to a boil over medium heat. Remove from heat and let cool. When cooled, skim off top and mix in sugar and vanilla. Return to heat and bring to a boil stirring constantly. Once boiling turn heat to medium and simmer for 20 minutes. Let cool and skim again.

In a large bowl beat egg yolks with mixer until thick (about 5 minutes). Keep mixer at low speed and gradually add cooled milk mixture. Stir in rum. Cover and refrigerate until cold, minimum 2 hours, best if served the next day.

To serve; pour egg nog in a glass and place one cinnamon stick in to stir.

MEXICAN HOT CHOCOLATE

INGREDIENTS:

• 4 cups milk

• 1 stick of cinnamon

• 2 tbsp. instant coffee granules

• 1/3 cup semi sweet chocolate chips

• 1/2 cup boiling water

• 2 tbsp. sugar

• 1/2 tsp. vanilla

DIRECTIONS:

Melt chocolate in boiling water. Add sugar, stirring until dissolved. Heat milk, cinnamon and coffee to boiling, remove cinnamon stick. Remove from heat and stir in chocolate mixture and vanilla. Serve immediately.

PIÑA COLADA

INGREDIENTS:

- 1/2 cup pineapple juice

- 3 ounces rum

- 1/4 cup canned cream of coconut

- 2 cups crushed ice

DIRECTIONS:

Pour pineapple juice, rum and cream of coconut in blender.
Add ice and blend until slushy. Serve in tall drink glasses
with a garnish wedge of fresh pineapple.

SANGRIA

INGREDIENTS:

- 1 cup sugar

- 1 cup water

- 1 liter dry red wine, chilled

- 2 oz. brandy

- 1 lime, thinly sliced

- 1 lemon, thinly sliced

- 1 orange, thinly sliced

- Juice of 1 orange

- 1 cup club soda, chilled

- Ice cubes

DIRECTIONS:

Boil water and add sugar, cooking until dissolved. Cool syrup. Combine wine, brandy, cooled syrup, orange juice, and sliced fruit in a large pitcher. Refrigerate for at least 1 hour. If made ahead do not add citrus slices until ready to serve. To serve, add club soda and pour over ice in tall glasses or large wine glasses. Add a few citrus slices to each glass.
Serves 6.

SPICY CITRUS DRINK

INGREDIENTS:

- 6 ripe tomatoes peeled and seeded

- 6 oranges; squeezed and juiced

- 2 Mexican limes; squeezed and juiced

- 1 medium sweet onion, finely chopped

- 4 small jalapeños seeded

- salt to taste

- Gold Tequila

DIRECTIONS:

Place all ingredients in a blender except the tequila. Blend until smooth and then refrigerate. Strain all seeds and pulp and pour into small drink glasses. Stir in 1 to 2 ounces tequila and enjoy this "HOT" refreshing drink.

ASS KICKIN'

TOMATO ICE

INGREDIENTS:

- 3 cups tomato juice

- 2 tbsp. onion, minced

- 2 tbsp. green chile, chopped

- 1 stalk celery, finely chopped

- 1 tbsp. lemon juice

- 3/4 tsp. salt

- 1/2 tsp. basil

- 2 to 4 dashes Ass Kickin'™ Roasted Garlic Hot Sauce or Ass Kickin'™ Original Hot Sauce

- 2 tbsp. parsley, minced

- Cilantro, for garnish.

DIRECTIONS:

In a medium sized sauce pan over medium heat, combine all the ingredients except the parsley and heat to boiling. Reduce heat and simmer, covered, for 5 minutes. Strain the mixture into an 8 inch square pan; stir in the parsley. Cover and freeze until solid.

When ready to serve, let the mixture stand at room temperature from 15 to 20 minutes, occasionally breaking it up with a spoon.

Place mixture in blender and process until mushy but not melted. Spoon mixture into sherbet or wine glasses. Garnish with sprigs of cilantro.
Serves 6.

18

VIRGIN MARY

(non-alcoholic)

INGREDIENTS:

• 1 (12 oz.) can tomato juice or V-8 juice

• Ass Kickin'™ Popcorn Seasoning, to taste

• 2 to 4 dashes Ass Kickin'™ Horseradish Hot Sauce or Tabasco

• Lemon wedges

• Celery stalks

• Ice

DIRECTIONS:

Combine first three ingredients. Pour over ice into tall glasses. Add celery stalk and lemon wedge. Serves 2.

ASS KICKIN'™

BREAD, TORTILLAS & PASTRIES

BLUE CORN TORTILLAS

INGREDIENTS:

- 2 cups blue corn meal

- 2 cups boiling water

- 1 tsp. salt

DIRECTIONS:

Gradually add corn meal to boiling, salted water. Stir thoroughly and let cool. Shape into very thin round cakes. Brown both sides on hot ungreased griddle.

BREAD PUFFS

INGREDIENTS:

- 2 cups flour

- 3 tbsp. baking powder

- 1 tsp. sugar

- 1/2 tsp. salt

- 1 tsp. Ass Kickin' Popcorn Seasoning

- 1 cup cold water

- Oil for frying; use Ass Kickin' Olive Oil to make your puffs really HOT!

DIRECTIONS:

Mix dry ingredients. Stir in water and mix dough until all the flour is wet. Dough will be sticky. Heat oil in skillet 1 inch deep. Drop heaping tablespoons full of dough into hot oil. Fry until golden brown, turning if necessary. Drain on paper towels and serve immediately.

CORN TORTILLAS

INGREDIENTS:

• 3 cups Masa Harina (Mexican ground cornmeal)

• 1 tbsp. shortening

• 1 tsp. salt

• 1 1/2 cups hot water - more if needed

DIRECTIONS:

Mix all ingredients thoroughly to stiff dough. Cover and set aside for 1/2 hour. Form into small balls and pat or roll into 6 inch rounds. Fry on both sides on a lightly oiled griddle.

CHILE CHEESE BREAD

INGREDIENTS:

- 3 cups self-rising flour

- 2 tbsp. sugar

- 1 (12 oz.) can warm beer

- 6 tbsp. melted butter or margarine

- 1 cup cheddar cheese, grated

- 1 (4 oz.) can chopped green chile, drained

Optional:
- **Mix in 2 tsp. Ass Kickin' Original Hot Sauce**

DIRECTIONS:

Mix flour and sugar together, add warm beer and mix. Stir in cheese, green chile and optional Ass Kickin'™ Original Hot Sauce. Pour into bread pan and pour melted butter over the top. Bake in 375° oven for 50 minutes.

24

CHILE CHEESE CORN BREAD

INGREDIENTS:

- 1 cup flour

- 1 cup cornmeal, white or yellow

- 1/4 cup sugar

- 1 tbsp. baking powder

- 1/2 tsp. salt

- 1 egg, beaten

- 1 cup milk

- 1/4 cup shortening or margarine, melted

- 1 cup cheddar cheese, grated

- 2 (4 oz.) cans green chile, chopped

Optional:

- 2 to 4 tsp. Ass Kickin'™ Original Hot sauce

DIRECTIONS:

Preheat oven to 425º. Combine flour, cornmeal, sugar, baking powder, and salt. Add beaten egg, optional Ass Kickin'™ Original Hot Sauce, milk, and melted shortening. Stir until mixture is just moist. Grease an 8 inch baking dish, spread half of the cheese over the bottom, top with green chile, and last half of the cheese. Pour the batter over the cheese-chile layer. Bake for 20 minutes or until done.

CHORIZO BREAD

INGREDIENTS:

- 1 loaf frozen bread dough

- 1 cup cheddar cheese grated

- 1/2 cup chorizo cooked and drained

- 1 (4 oz) can chopped green chiles

- 1 tbsp. Ass Kickin' Roasted Garlic Hot Sauce (optional)

- 1 egg beaten

- 3 tbsp. melted butter

DIRECTIONS:

Thaw frozen bread dough. Roll or stretch bread dough on a greased cookie sheet until it reaches a 6 X 12" rectangle. Set aside. Combine cheese, chorizo, chilies and egg and Ass Kickin' Hot Sauce. Spread filling on top of dough and roll jelly-roll fashion. Leave on greased cookie sheet and let rise until double in size. Pre-heat oven to 375°. Brush top of loaf with butter and bake at 375° for 20 minutes.

FLOUR TORTILLAS

INGREDIENTS:

- **6 cups flour**

- **2 tsp. salt**

- **3/4 cup shortening**

- **2 to 2 1/4 cups water**

DIRECTIONS:

Cut shortening into flour and salt. Add water, 1/2 cup at a time, stirring with a fork until dough comes together. Knead dough until soft and smooth. You may need to add more water if dough is too dry or more flour if dough is too sticky. Knead dough for about 5 minutes. Cover and let rest for 30 minutes. Pinch off walnut size piece of dough and roll into a circle. Do a few at time to stay ahead as tortillas are cooking. Place uncooked tortilla on a hot, ungreased griddle until edges appear dry and underside is starting to brown. Turn tortilla and continue cooking. Remove to plate covered with a towel to keep warm. Makes 3 dozen tortillas.

Keep unused tortillas in a sealable, plastic bag in the refrigerator. To reheat, place on hot griddle, wrap in foil and place in warm oven, or heat for 15 seconds in the microwave oven.

GARLIC BREAD

INGREDIENTS:

• 1 loaf french bread

• 1 tbsp. garlic powder

• 1/4 cup finely chopped parsley or 1 tbsp. dried parsley flakes

• 1 tbsp. Ass Kickin' Popcorn Seasoning

• 1 stick butter or margarine

  1 cup parmesan cheese

DIRECTIONS:

Slice bread into 1" diagonal slices or slice in half lengthwise. Melt butter in a small sauce pan, add garlic, parsley and Ass Kickin' Popcorn Seasoning and mix well.
Brush butter evenly over bread and sprinkle with parmesan cheese.

Wrap bread in foil and place on a cookie sheet. Bake at 250^0 for 1/2 hour, open foil and bake an additional 10 minutes.

INDIAN FRY BREAD

INGREDIENTS:

- **3 cups flour**

- **1 1/2 tsp. baking powder**

- **1/2 tsp. salt**

- **1 1/3 cups warm water**

Optional:

- **Ass Kickin'™ Olive Oil**

DIRECTIONS:

Mix the flour, baking powder, and salt. Add the water and knead the dough until soft. Divide dough into 4 equal portions and roll dough to 1/4 inch thick rounds.

Fry bread in 2 inches of Ass Kickin'™ Olive Oil or your favorite vegetable oil until puffed and lightly browned on both sides, turning only once. Drain on absorbent paper.

May be eaten alone, sprinkled with cinnamon sugar, drizzled with honey, or used as the base for Navajo Tacos (pg. 104). Great with anything from soup to stew.

MEXICAN CORN BREAD

INGREDIENTS:

- 1 1/2 cups cornmeal
- 2 eggs
- 1 cup sharp cheese, grated
- 1/4 tsp. baking soda - add to buttermilk
- 1 cup buttermilk
- 3 tbsp. oil or heat it up with 3 tbsp. Ass Kickin'™ Olive Oil
- 1/2 tsp. salt
- 1 can cream style corn
- 1 (4oz.) can chopped green chile or 5 fresh green chile, roasted, peeled and seeded
- 2 tsp. baking powder

Optional: chopped green bell pepper, pimentos, crumbled bacon, garlic salt.

DIRECTIONS:

Combine ingredients and pour into a well greased, hot, 9 x 13" pan. Bake 25 to 30 minutes in a 400° oven.

SOFT PRETZELS

INGREDIENTS:

• 2 cups warm water

• 2 envelopes dry yeast

• 1/2 cup butter or margarine, softened

• 1 egg

• 6 1/2 to 7 1/2 cups flour

• 1/2 cup sugar

• 2 tsp. salt

• 1 egg yolk

• 1 tbsp. water

• Ass Kickin' Popcorn Seasoning or coarse salt

DIRECTIONS:

Measure warm water into large warm bowl. Sprinkle in yeast and stir until dissolved. Add sugar, salt, butter, egg and 3 cups flour. Beat until smooth. Add enough additional flour to make dough stiff. Cover bowl tightly with foil. Refrigerate 2 to 24 hours. Turn dough out onto lightly floured board. Divide in half. Cut each half into 16 equal pieces. Roll each piece into a pencil shape, 16 to 20 inches long.

Shape into pretzels. Place on lightly greased baking sheets. Blend egg yolk with 2 tbsp. water. Brush pretzels with egg yolk mixture. Sprinkle with Ass Kickin' Popcorn Seasoning or coarse salt. Let rise until doubled; about 25 minutes. Bake at 400° about 15 minutes.
Remove from baking sheets and cool on wire racks.
Makes 32 pretzels.

SOPAPILLAS

(Mexican Fried Bread)

INGREDIENTS:

- 2 cups flour

- 2 tsp. baking powder

- 1/2 tsp. salt

- 4 tbsp. shortening

- 1/2 cup water, little more if needed

- Hot oil, (Ass Kickin'™ Olive Oil really heats em up!!)

DIRECTIONS:

Combine flour, baking powder and salt in bowl. Cut in short-ening, add water, and mix to a stiff dough. Knead thorough-ly on lightly floured board. Cover with cloth and set aside for 15 minutes. On floured board roll out quite thin. Cut out dough into rounds, squares, or diamonds. Fry a few at a time in 2 inches of oil, turning several times. Bread will puff in frying. Serve plain as a bread, with honey, or roll in cinnamon and sugar.

TORTILLA CHEESE CRISP

INGREDIENTS:

• Large flour tortilla

• Cheddar cheese (or preference)

• Top with any of our Ass Kickin'™ Salsas.
  Original Ass Kickin'™ Salsa, Ass Kickin'™ Whiskey
  Peppercorn, Roasted Green Chile and Tequila or
  Peach Rum Salsas

DIRECTIONS:

Place large flour tortilla on heated griddle. Butter tortilla and cover with grated cheese. Place under broiler until cheese melts. Use a pizza cutter and slice. Pass the Ass Kickin'™ salsa and serve immediately.

DESSERTS

ASS KICKIN'™

BISCOCHITOS
(Cookies)

INGREDIENTS:

- **2 cups butter or margarine**
- **1/4 cup cold water**
- **1 cup sugar**
- **2 well beaten eggs**
- **1/4 cup whiskey**
- **6 cups flour**
- **1 tsp. salt**
- **1 tbsp. baking powder**
- **1 tsp. anise seed**

DIRECTIONS:

Blend butter and sugar together in large bowl. Stir in eggs, water, and whiskey. Add flour, baking powder, salt, and anise seed. Roll on a floured board to 1/8 inch thickness. Cut with cookie cutters and place on lightly greased cookie sheet. Brush with melted butter then sprinkle with cinnamon and sugar. Bake in 350° oven for 7 to 8 minutes. Watch carefully so as not to burn.

CHILE PEANUT BRITTLE

INGREDIENTS:

- 1 cup unsalted peanuts or Ass Kickin'™ Peanuts

- 1/4 cup flaked coconut

- 1 tsp. vegetable oil

- 2 tsp. red chile powder

- 1 cup sugar

- 1/2 cup light corn syrup

- 1 tsp. butter or margarine

- 1 tsp. baking soda

DIRECTIONS:

Combine peanuts, coconut, oil, and chile powder in a glass pie plate. Microwave on high for 2 minutes, stirring after 1 minute. Set aside.

Grease a baking sheet. Combine sugar and corn syrup in a 5 quart bowl and microwave on high for 6 minutes, stir after 3 minutes. Mix in butter and cook 1 minute on high. Immediately stir in baking soda. Add peanut mixture and stir until light and foamy. Pour mixture onto greased baking sheet. Flatten candy with hands or greased rolling pin - be careful it is hot! Let peanut brittle stand until cool and then break into pieces.

CHOCOLATE CHIMICHANGA

INGREDIENTS:

• **Flour tortillas**

• **Large sweet or semisweet chocolate bar with or without almonds**

• **Oil for frying or try Ass Kickin'™ Olive Oil for an Ass Kickin'™ chimi!**

DIRECTIONS:

Break up chocolate bar into 2 x 1 inch chunks. Wrap each piece of chocolate in 1/4 pie shaped portion of flour tortilla, starting from point and roll, tucking in sides to completely enclose chocolate. Secure with tooth pick.

Fry in hot oil or hot Ass Kickin'™ Olive Oil until lightly browned. Drain on absorbent paper. Dust with powdered sugar. Best eaten while still warm.

EASY CARAMEL FLAN

Pour sugar into a buttered 9 x 9" pan. Pour blended custard over caramel. Place in pan of water and bake 45 to 60 minutes in a 350° oven. Remove from oven, cool, and refrigerate at least 3 hours. Invert onto a platter or spoon out individual servings. Serves 9.

INGREDIENTS:

• 1 can condensed milk

• 1 1/2 cups milk

• 4 eggs

• 1 tsp. vanilla

• 1/4 cup sugar

• 1 cup sugar for caramelizing

DIRECTIONS:

Blend condensed milk, eggs, vanilla, and 1/4 cup sugar together in a blender for 1 minute. Place 1 cup sugar in cast iron skillet or heavy sauce pan and heat over medium heat until sugar is melted and brown.

EMPANADAS

INGREDIENTS:

- 2 cups flour

- 2 tbsp. sugar

- 2 tsp. baking powder

- 1/2 tsp. salt

- 1/3 cup shortening

- 1/3 cup cold water

- Oil for frying

DIRECTIONS:

Combine flour, sugar, baking powder, and salt. Cut in shortening and add water to make stiff dough. Roll on floured board and cut into 4 inch rounds. Place 1 to 2 tbsp. filling on half of round. Wet edges and press with fork to seal. Fry in hot oil or Ass Kickin'™ Olive Oil, turning once, until golden brown. Drain on absorbent paper. Dust with powdered sugar if desired.

Filling: Use prepared pie filling or fresh fruit sweetened with sugar and cinnamon.

FLAN
(CARAMEL PUDDING)

INGREDIENTS:

• 1 1/2 quarts milk

• 5 eggs

• 1/2 tsp. salt

• 1 1/2 cups sugar

• 1 tsp. vanilla

DIRECTIONS:

Over low heat melt 1/2 cup sugar in skillet until a light brown syrup forms. Spread evenly in sides and bottom of a 9 inch pie pan or 8 individual custard cups while still hot. Beat eggs until light and frothy. Gradually add 1 cup sugar to eggs. Stir in milk, salt and vanilla. Pour into pie pan or custard cups containing burnt sugar. Set in larger pan containing enough boiling water to come half way up side of pie pan or cups and bake in 350° oven for about 15 to 25 minutes depending on size you are making. To check for doneness, insert knife blade in center.

If it comes out clean, or when a very shallow crevice forms when center of custard is pushed with the back of a spoon, it is done.

Remove dish from hot water. Cool, cover and refrigerate at least 3 hours. To unmold, loosen edge of flan with a knife; cover dish with a rimmed plate and invert quickly.

MEXICAN CHOCOLATE COOKIES

INGREDIENTS:

- 1/2 cup butter or margarine, softened

- 1 cup sugar

- 1 egg, beaten

- 1 tsp. vanilla

- 1 cup flour

- 2 tbsp. unsweetened cocoa

- 1/2 tsp. each, baking powder and cinnamon

- 1/3 cup finely chopped pecans or Ass Kickin'™ Peanuts

DIRECTIONS:

Cream butter and sugar, blend in egg and vanilla. Add flour, baking powder and cinnamon. Stir in pecans or Ass Kickin'™ Peanuts. Form into roll and wrap in wax paper. Refrigerate 1 to 2 hours. Slice dough 1/4 inch thick, and bake at 325° for 15 to 18 minutes. Let cool on pan for a few minutes before placing on rack.

MEXICAN CHOCOLATE ICE CREAM

INGREDIENTS:

- 7 oz. semisweet chocolate

- 1 tsp. ground cinnamon

- 3/4 cup sugar

- 1 quart half and half

- 2 large eggs, beaten

- 2 tsp. vanilla

Optional
- Ass Kickin'™ Peanut Brittle

DIRECTIONS:

Chop chocolate and put in 3 quart saucepan, add cinnamon, over very low heat stir until smoothly melted. Add sugar, half and half, and eggs. Increase heat to medium-low and stir mixture until it coats the back of a metal spoon evenly, 20 to 30 minutes. Stir in vanilla. Remove from heat and cool. Refrigerate covered until cold, at least 3 hours or overnight. Pour mixture into an ice cream freezer (1 1/2-quart size or bigger). Freeze according to manufacturer's directions until firm. Serve immediately or place in freezer covered until ready to use.

* For some crunchy hot ice cream top with crumbled Ass Kickin'™ Peanut Brittle

MEXICAN WEDDING CAKES

INGREDIENTS:

- 2 cups flour

- 1 cup butter (best) or margarine

- 3/4 cup sugar

- 1/4 tsp. salt

- 2 tsp. vanilla or almond flavoring

- 2 tbsp. water

- 1 cup almonds or pecans, finely chopped

- Powdered sugar

DIRECTIONS:

Cream butter and sugar together, add water and vanilla. Stir in flour, salt, and nuts and mix thoroughly. Form into 1 inch balls. Flatten balls slightly. Bake on ungreased cookie sheet in 275° oven for 30 to 40 minutes or until lightly brown. Remove to cooling rack and dust heavily with powdered sugar.

MICROWAVE PRALINES #1

INGREDIENTS:

- 1 lb. box light brown sugar

- 1/2 pint whipping cream

- 1 1/2 tsp. vanilla

- 1/2 stick margarine (4 tbsp.)

- 2 cups pecan halves

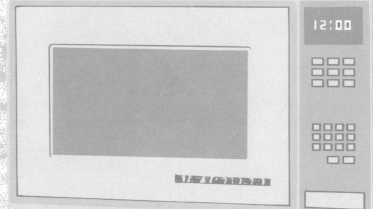

DIRECTIONS:

Mix brown sugar and cream in large, microwave safe bowl. Cook on high for 12 minutes. Stir and add vanilla and margarine. Microwave 2 minutes more. Add pecans, stir and microwave 2 minutes longer. Drop by spoonfuls onto wax paper or oil sprayed aluminum foil.

MICROWAVE PRALINES #2

When candy reaches soft-ball stage, cool and then beat with a wooden spoon until candy thickens. Stir in pecans and drop by spoonfuls on greased cookie sheet or wax paper. Store in airtight container.

INGREDIENTS:

• 1/2 cup dark brown sugar

• 1 1/2 cups Eagle Brand Sweetened Condensed Milk

• 1 tsp. baking soda

• Dash of salt

• 1 tsp. vanilla

• 1 cup pecan halves

DIRECTIONS:

Combine condensed milk, brown sugar, baking soda, and salt in a 5 quart glass bowl and mix thoroughly. Microwave on high 10 to 11 minutes or until candy reaches a soft-ball stage (235°F).

PECAN PRALINES

INGREDIENTS:

- 1 cup dark brown sugar

- 1 cup white sugar

- 1/2 cup half and half

- 3 tbsp. butter

- 1 cup whole pecan halves

DIRECTIONS:

Boil sugar and cream to a thread state (228°) stirring often. Add butter and pecans. Cook to soft ball stage. Remove from heat. Cool to lukewarm. Beat until thickened. Drop from spoon on to wax paper. Store in air tight container or in refrigerator.

PIÑON CRESCENTS

Bake in a 275° oven for 25 to 30 minutes or until edges are lightly browned. Remove cookies from pan and place on rack. Dust with powdered sugar while still warm.

INGREDIENTS:

- **1 cup butter or margarine at room temperature**

- **1/4 cups powdered sugar**

- **2 tsp. vanilla**

- **2 cups all-purpose flour**

- **1 cup pinons or pine nuts, finely chopped**

- **Powdered sugar for dusting**

DIRECTIONS:

In a bowl, beat butter, powdered sugar, and vanilla until creamy. Stir in flour and piñons until well mixed. Pinch off a walnut size piece of dough and roll between hands to form rope shape. Place on ungreased baking sheet and shape into a crescent.

47

ASS KICKIN'™

EGGS AND CHEESE

BREAKFAST SANDWICH

DIRECTIONS:

Heat oil in skillet and fry eggs, when cooked to your liking top with cheese and turn stove off. Place each egg on hamburger bun and then top with Ass Kickin' Roasted Garlic Hot Sauce. Serve with Papas con Chile Verde (pg. 190) and fresh cantaloupe. Serves 2 to 4.

INGREDIENTS:

- **4 large eggs**

- **4 hamburger buns**

- **4 slices American cheese**

- **Ass Kickin' Olive Oil**

- **Ass Kickin' Roasted Garlic Hot Sauce**

COMPANY OMELET

INGREDIENTS:

• 5 slices bread (any kind), with crusts removed

• Butter or margarine

• 3/4 lb. longhorn or cheddar cheese, grated

• 1 (4oz.) can chopped green chile

• 4 eggs, beaten

• 2 cups milk

• Salt to taste

• 1/2 tsp. dry mustard

• Ass Kickin'™ Salsa to taste

DIRECTIONS:

Butter bread and place in 9 inch baking dish. Cover with grated cheese and green chile. Combine remaining ingredients and pour over bread, cheese and chile. Let stand in the refrigerator overnight. Cover and bake 1 hour at 325°. Remove cover and bake 5 minutes or until puffy and set.
Pass the Ass Kickin'™ Salsa.
Serves 4 to 6.

CHILE CHEESE BAKE

INGREDIENTS:

- 1 can diced green chile, or 4-6 roasted, peeled green chiles diced

- 1 can (4 oz.) mushrooms, drained

- 1 pound monterey jack cheese coarsely grated

- 1 pound sharp cheddar cheese coarsely grated

- 4 eggs, separated

- 2/3 cup evaporated milk, undiluted

- 1 tbsp. flour

- 2 medium tomatoes, sliced

- 2 tsp. Ass Kickin'™ Roasted Garlic Hot Sauce Optional to make this an Ass Kickin'™ chile cheese bake!

- Salt and pepper to taste

DIRECTIONS:

Toss together green chile, mushrooms and cheese. Turn into well greased casserole. Beat egg whites to stiff peaks. Combine yolks, flour, milk, seasonings, Ass Kickin'™ Roasted Garlic Hot Sauce and blend until smooth. Fold in whites. Pour over cheese mixture and "ooze" in with fork. Bake 350° for 30 minutes. Arrange tomato slices around edges and bake an additional 30 minutes or until an inserted knife comes out clean. Serves 8-10.

DEVILED EGGS

INGREDIENTS:

- 6 hard boiled eggs

- 1/4 cup mayonnaise

- 1/2 tsp salt

- 1/3 cup chopped tomatoes

- 1 tsp. chili powder or Ass Kickin' Popcorn Seasoning

DIRECTIONS:

Remove shells from eggs and slice them in half lengthwise.
Carefully remove yolks and place them in a bowl. Mash
finely with a fork. Add mayonnaise, salt, tomatoes, and
Ass Kickin' Popcorn Seasoning, blend gently. Using a
spoon, pile egg yolk mixture into center of egg white
halves. Cover and refrigerate until you are ready to serve.

EGG SALAD SANDWICHES

DIRECTIONS:

Mix all ingredients until well blended. Place a generous helping on a slice of bread and spread evenly, top with 2nd slice of bread and enjoy. Mixture makes 2 cups. Serve with side of Ass Kickin' Corn Chips.

INGREDIENTS:

- 6 hard boiled eggs, chopped

- 1/4 cup minced onion

- 1/2 cup mayonnaise

- 3 tbsp. prepared mustard (use Ass Kickin' Mustard it's great!)

- 1 tsp. salt

FRITTATA

INGREDIENTS:

- 6 eggs

- 1 cup milk

- 1 tbsp. butter, melted

- 1/4 tsp. salt

- 1/4 tsp. pepper

- 2 cloves garlic chopped

- 1 cup grated cheddar cheese

DIRECTIONS:

Beat first 6 ingredients with a fork or wire whisk until blended. Pour into a greased 10" pie dish (the deeper the better). Sprinkle cheese over the top. Bake at 400° for 20 minutes or until firm and set and lightly browned.
Top with any of your favorite Ass Kickin' Salsas for a real Ass Kickin' Frittata.

GREEN CHILE EGG SCRAMBLE

INGREDIENTS:

- 6 eggs

- 1/2 tsp. salt

- 1 (4oz) can diced green chilies

- 1 clove Ass Kickin' garlic chopped (or one fresh)

- 1/4 cup sliced mushrooms

- 2 tsp. butter or oil

DIRECTIONS:

Beat eggs, then add salt, mushrooms, garlic and green chilies, mix lightly. Heat skillet and add butter or oil, when hot add egg mixture. Stir eggs from bottom, and serve immediately when cooked to desired texture. Top with your favorite Ass Kickin' Hot Sauce.

GREEN CHILE OMELET

INGREDIENTS:

- 1 lb. monterey jack cheese, grated

- 1 lb. cheddar cheese, grated

- 1 pint sour cream

- 2 (4oz.) cans chopped green chile

- 1 dozen eggs

- **Ass Kickin'™ Roasted Green Chile & Tequila Salsa**

DIRECTIONS:

Beat eggs together, add 1/2 of total cheese, sour cream, and chiles. Put rest of cheese in bottom of 10" x 14" pan. Pour egg mixture on top and bake 45 minutes at 350°. Let set 5 to 10 minutes before serving. Serves a large group. Top with Ass Kickin'™ Green Chile & Tequila Salsa or any other of your favorite salsas.

56

GREEN CHILE QUICHE

INGREDIENTS:

- **Pie crust for 10 inch pie plate**

- **4 eggs**

- **1 1/2 cup monterey jack cheese, grated**

- **1 cup cheddar cheese, grated**

- **1 (4 oz.) can chopped green chiles, drained**

- **1 cup half and half**

- **2 green onions, chopped, including tops**

- **Dash of cumin**

Optional:

- **4 to 5 dashes of Ass Kickin'™ Hot Sauce**

DIRECTIONS:

Fit crust in pie pan and flute edges. Prick bottom and sides of shell with a fork and bake in 400° oven about 12 minutes or until golden brown. Reduce heat to 325°.

Sprinkle cheeses over baked pie crust. Evenly distribute the chiles over the cheese. Beat eggs in a medium-size bowl, add half and half, cumin, and hot sauce stirring to blend and pour over the chiles. Bake about 40 minutes or until center of pie appears set when the pan is gently shaken. Let stand at least 5 minutes before cutting. Serve warm or at room temperature.

ASS KICKIN'™

GREEN CHILE CHEESE CASSEROLE

INGREDIENTS:

- 2 cans whole or diced green chiles or 8-10 fresh roasted green chiles

- 2 cups milk

- 5 tbsp. margarine, melted

- 1 pound sharp cheddar cheese, grated

- 1 cup cracker crumbs

- 1/2 tsp. salt or Ass Kickin'™ Popcorn Seasoning

- 4 eggs

DIRECTIONS:

Alternate layers of chile and cheese in greased casserole dish saving some cheese for the top. Beat together eggs, milk, and Ass Kickin'™ Popcorn Seasoning. Add cracker crumbs to melted margarine and mix until moistened. Pour egg mixture over chile and cheese, sprinkle with cheese and buttered cracker crumbs. Bake at 325° for 1 hour. Serves 6-8.

HAM & CHEESE STRATA

INGREDIENTS:

- **12 slices of white bread**

- **1 1/2 cups cheddar cheese shredded**

- **1 (10oz) package frozen chopped broccoli**

- **1 cup chopped ham**

- **1/2 cup chopped onion**

- **2 cloves Ass Kickin' or fresh garlic minced**

- **1 (8oz) package cream cheese, softened**

- **3 eggs**

- **1 cup milk**

DIRECTIONS:

Place 6 slices of bread on the bottom of a 12x8" baking dish. Cover with 1 cup cheddar cheese, thawed and drained broccoli, onion, Ass Kickin'™ Garlic, and ham. Beat cream cheese until light and fluffy, add eggs one at a time blending well after each one. Stir in milk and set aside. Place remaining bread slices diagonally and place on top of ham & vegetables. Top bread with cream cheese & egg mixture and then top with remaining cheese.

Bake at 350° for 45-50 minutes. Let stand 10 minutes before cutting.

ASS KICKIN'™

MEXICAN OMELET

INGREDIENTS:

• 1 avocado, chopped

• 1/2 cup sour cream

• 2 green chiles, chopped

• 2 green onions, chopped

• 1/4 lemon, juiced

• Ass Kickin'™ Hot Sauce to taste

• 2 tbsp. butter or margarine

• 6 beaten eggs

• 1/4 lb. monterey jack cheese, grated

DIRECTIONS:

Preheat oven to 325°. Combine avocado, sour cream, chile, onion, lemon juice and Ass Kickin'™ Hot Sauce and set aside. Melt butter in ovenproof pan, add beaten eggs and cook 3 to 5 minutes, moving cooked egg to center allowing uncooked portions to flow to bottom of pan. (Eggs will continue to cook while in the oven). Put pan in oven and cook 3 to 4 minutes.

Cover half of eggs with the cheese and return to oven 3 to 4 minutes, or until cheese melts. Remove from oven and cover other half with avocado mixture and return to oven for 4 to 5 minutes or until hot. Remove from oven, fold omelet in half, and gently remove from pan. Pass the Ass Kickin'™ Hot Sauce or Ass Kickin'™ Salsa! Serves 4.

POACHED EGGS WITH NOPALITOS

INGREDIENTS:

• 1 (15oz) jar nopalitos (cactus)

• 6 flour tortillas

• 2 cups shredded cheddar cheese

• 2 cups chopped tomatoes

• 1 (13 oz) jar Ass Kickin'™ Roasted Green Chile & Tequila Salsa

• 6 poached eggs

DIRECTIONS:

Place tortillas directly on oven rack and bake at 350º until crisp and lightly browned. Remove from oven and place on cookie sheets, top with cheese, nopalitos and tomatoes. Return to oven and bake until cheese melts. Place an egg on top of each tortilla. Spoon salsa over each serving.

SALSA Huevos Rancheros

(Ranch style sauce for eggs)

INGREDIENTS:

- 8 slices bacon, cut into small pieces

- 1 (13oz.) jar Ass Kickin'™ Salsa

- Corn tortillas

- Grated cheese

DIRECTIONS:

Fry the bacon pieces slowly until almost done; remove, drain and clean pan. Place Ass Kickin'™ Salsa with fried bacon back in pan and simmer while cooking eggs. If sauce is too thick add a little water.

Serve sauce over eggs cooked to your liking (fried, poached, scrambled). Place eggs on heated or fried tortillas cover with sauce and grated cheese.

ASS KICKIN'™
ENTREES

ARROZ SOPA

(RICE SOUP)

INGREDIENTS:

- 1 cup uncooked rice

- 2 quarts beef or chicken broth

- Sprig of fresh mint, minced

- 1/4 tsp. oregano

- 1 small green pepper, chopped

- 3 tbsp. oil

- 1 large can tomatoes

- 1/3 cup celery, chopped

- 1 clove garlic, minced

- Dash Ass Kickin'™ Hot Sauce or another favorite

DIRECTIONS:

Heat oil and brown rice in a heavy saucepan. Add onion, green pepper, celery, garlic, tomatoes, spices and dash of hot sauce. Simmer for 10 minutes over low heat. Add broth, cover and cook for 1 to 1 1/2 hours. Sprinkle with grated parmesan cheese. Serves 6.

ARROZ CON POLLO

(CHICKEN with RICE)

INGREDIENTS:

- 1 frying chicken (2-3 lb) cut up or 6 chicken breasts

- 2 cups long grain rice (not minute rice)

- 2 cans chicken broth or 3 cups chicken bouillon

- 2 medium onions, diced

- 2 cloves garlic, use minced Ass Kickin'™ Garlic for "*real*" heat

- 2 medium tomatoes, diced or 1 (15oz.) can tomatoes

- 2 sprigs cilantro (Mexican parsley), minced

- 1 small jar Spanish olives

- 1 box frozen peas, optional

DIRECTIONS:

Brown chicken in oil and drain. Place in 9 x 12" baking dish and add rice, onion, Ass Kickin'™ Garlic, olives, tomato, and cilantro. Cover with broth and bake 1 hour at 350º, adding peas last 15 minutes.

ALBONDIGAS SOUP

(Meatball soup)

INGREDIENTS:

- 4 green onions, chopped

- 1 clove Ass Kickin'™ Garlic, minced

- 1/4 tsp. ground coriander

- 1/4 tsp. oregano

- Sprig of fresh mint, minced

- 1 tomato, chopped

- 2 quarts beef broth

- Olive oil

DIRECTIONS:

Heat oil (or Ass Kickin'™ Olive Oil to spice up your soup) and sauté onions, Ass Kickin'™ Garlic, tomato, and spices over medium heat for about 5 minutes. Add broth and simmer for 30 minutes. (See "Meatball Ingredients below")

MEATBALL INGREDIENTS:

- 1 1/2 lb. lean ground round steak

- 1/3 cup uncooked rice

- 1 cup tomato puree

- 2 green onions, chopped

- 1/4 tsp. oregano

- Salt and pepper to taste

DIRECTIONS:

Combine meat, rice, tomato puree, onion, and seasonings. Shape into balls and drop into soup. Cover and simmer for 30 minutes.

BARBECUED CHICKEN

INGREDIENTS:

- 1 3 to 4 lb. frying chicken, cut up

- Barbecue sauce:
    1/2 cup margarine
    1/4 cup lemon juice
    2 tbsp. horseradish
    2 tbsp. vinegar
    2 tbsp. ketchup or Ass Kickin'™ Ketchup
    1 tsp. salt
    2 tsp. worcestershire sauce
    1 tsp. Ass Kickin'™ Chicken Wing Sauce or
      Tabasco

DIRECTIONS:

Combine all sauce ingredients in a small sauce pan and heat until margarine has melted.

Grill chicken over medium hot coals 40 to 50 minutes, turning as needed to brown evenly. Baste with sauce last 10 minutes of cooking. Extra sauce is great for the table.

BARBECUED BEEF OR PORK RIBS

INGREDIENTS:

• 3 lbs. of beef or pork ribs

• 2 large cans pickled jalapeños

DIRECTIONS:

Marinate the ribs in the refrigerator in the juice from the jalapeños along with some of the jalapenos for 24 hours. Drain the ribs and grill, covered over medium coals for 1 1/2 to 2 hours until done. Baste the ribs with the marinade while cooking. Turn as needed. Serve with mango pineapple salsa (pg. 156) or a jar of Ass Kickin'™ Peach Rum Salsa.

ASS KICKIN'

BARBECUED BRISKET

INGREDIENTS:

• 1 whole brisket

• Marinade:
   2 1/2 cups ketchup (or Ass Kickin'™ Ketchup for a real kick!)
   3/4 cup brown sugar
   1 1/2 cups Red Chile Sauce (pg. 106)
   1 1/2 cups water
   1 can beer
   3/4 cup lemon juice
   1/2 cup prepared mustard
   1 tbsp. celery seed
   4 tbsp. worcestershire sauce
   2 tbsp. soy sauce
   4 to 6 cloves garlic, minced or Ass Kickin'™ Garlic

Optional:

• Dash of Ass Kickin'™ Hot Sauce

DIRECTIONS:

Combine marinade ingredients. Trim the brisket of as much fat as possible. Using a fork, poke holes in the brisket so that it will absorb the marinade. A plastic bag works well to hold the brisket and the marinade. Refrigerate the brisket and marinate overnight.

Place brisket on hot grill to sear the meat. Then in a disposable foil pan, cover tightly with foil and return to the grill. Close the hood and cook on slow coals for about 4 hours. You may want to turn the meat midway through cooking. This marinade may be used as a sauce for the cooked meat, but be sure to heat it to boiling before serving. Slice the meat across the grain.

BORDER BEANS

INGREDIENTS:

- 2 lbs. dry pinto beans

- Salt pork - 1 small cube

- 3 or 4 cloves garlic, minced - Make 'em Ass Kickin'™ border beans using Ass Kickin'™ Garlic

- 1 tbsp. dried oregano

- 4 to 8 chile pequins or serranos or Ass Kickin'™ Hot Sauce, to taste

- Salt to taste

DIRECTIONS:

Wash and sort beans. Put beans and enough water to cover by 4 inches in a heavy 6 quart sauce pan and bring to boil. Lower heat to a simmer and add rest of ingredients. Cook 4 to 6 hours stirring occasionally; add boiling water as needed until beans are tender. Do not add salt until beans are done or they will be tough. Beans will thicken the longer they are cooked. Serve with Ass Kickin'™ Corn Bread or flour tortillas.

CAJUN CATFISH

INGREDIENTS:

- 1 1/2 lbs catfish fillets

- 2/3 cup lemon Juice

- 2 tsp. Ass Kickin'™ Cajun Hot Sauce or another Cajun Hot Sauce

- 2/3 cup flour

- 2/3 cup yellow cornmeal

- 1 tsp. salt

- Vegetable Oil

DIRECTIONS:

In a shallow dish combine lemon juice and Ass Kickin'™ Cajun Hot Sauce. Place fish in dish, turn over in sauce and refrigerate for 1 hour, turning occasionally. Mix flour, cornmeal and salt together and place on wax paper or a paper plate. Remove fish from refrigerator and coat each piece with flour mixture.

In a large skillet heat 1" vegetable oil until approximately 350°. Fry fish 3 to 5 minutes each until golden brown on both sides. Drain on paper towels and serve with additional Ass Kickin'™ Cajun Hot Sauce.

CHEESE ENCHILADAS

INGREDIENTS:

• 1 dozen corn tortillas

• 1 lb. grated longhorn or cheddar cheese

• 1 medium onion

• 1 large can enchilada sauce or 3 cups Red Chile Sauce (pg. 161)

• Oil for frying

• Shredded lettuce

• Diced tomatoes

Optional:

• Sour cream

DIRECTIONS:

Soften tortillas in hot enchilada sauce or fry in hot Ass Kickin'™ Olive Oil or another of your favorite oils until soft (10 to 15 seconds and drain on absorbent paper). Fill each with cheese and diced onion roll and put in 9 x 12" baking dish seam side down. Pour sauce over tortillas and sprinkle with reserved cheese. Bake in 350º oven for 30 minutes or until hot and bubbly. Serve with shredded lettuce, diced tomatoes, and sour cream. Serves 4 to 6.

CHALUPAS

INGREDIENTS:

- 4-5 lb. pork roast, well trimmed

- 2 jalapeño peppers

- 4 cloves garlic or Ass Kickin'™ Garlic (optional), minced

- 1 1/2 tbsp. oregano

- 2 to 4 tbsp. chile powder, or to taste

- 1 1/2 tsp. comino seeds or ground cumin

- 2 lbs. pinto beans, washed and sorted

- Salt and pepper to taste

- Ass Kickin'™ Corn Chips

- Ass Kickin'™ Salsa

- Shredded lettuce

- Grated cheese

- Chopped tomatoes

- Chopped onions

- Diced avocado

- Sour cream

DIRECTIONS:

Combine first 8 ingredients in a large, heavy Dutch oven with enough water to cover. Bring to a boil, reduce heat, stir often and simmer 6-8 hours, adding boiling water as needed to cover mixture. After 4 hours the meat will begin to fall apart. Remove bone and large chunks of pork. Discard excess fat and shred large chunks of pork. Return to pan and continue cooking until mixture thickens.

To serve - crush a pile of Ass Kickin'™ Corn Chips and top with meat and bean mixture, cheese, lettuce, tomato, onion, avocado, Ass Kickin'™ Salsa, and sour cream.
Serves 8-10.

CHEESEBURGER PIE

INGREDIENTS:

- 1 (9") unbaked pastry shell

- 8 pieces sliced American cheese cut into 1" slices

- 1 lb lean ground beef

- 1/2 cup tomato sauce

- 1/3 cup chopped green pepper

- 1/3 cup chopped onion

- 1 tsp. beef bouillon cube

- 3 eggs; beaten

- 2 tbsp. flour

- 2 tbsp. Ass Kickin' Olive Oil

- optional: chopped tomato, shredded lettuce and Ass Kickin' Salsa

DIRECTIONS:

Pre-heat oven to 425º. Prick pastry shell and bake 8 minutes, remove from oven. Reduce oven to 350º. In a large skillet, brown meat in Olive Oil, and drain. In same skillet with beef, add tomato sauce, green pepper, onion and bouillon cube, stir until bouillon dissolves. Remove from heat, stir in eggs, flour and 1/2 of cheese slices. Pour into pastry shell and bake 25 minutes.

Remove from oven, place remaining cheese slices on top of pie and return to oven for 5 minutes or until cheese melts.

CHEESE SOUP

INGREDIENTS:

• 1/4 cup butter or margarine

• 1/2 cup onion, chopped

• 1 clove Ass Kickin'™ Garlic or fresh garlic, minced

• 1/2 cup flour

• 1/2 tsp. cumin

• 1 quart milk, scalded

• 1 can chicken broth

• 1 large tomato, chopped

• 1 (4 oz.) can chopped green chile

• 4 ounces sharp cheddar cheese, grated

• 4 ounces monterey jack cheese, grated

• Salt and pepper to taste

DIRECTIONS:

In a large saucepan, melt butter, saute onion and Ass Kickin'™ garlic until tender. Add flour, cumin, salt and pepper, stirring constantly for 1 minute. Whisk in scalded milk and broth, stirring often on low heat for 5 minutes. Add tomato and chiles. Heat through. Remove from heat and stir in cheddar and jack cheese until melted. Makes about 8 cups. Serve with warmed tortilla chips.

CHICKEN TAQUITOS

(rolled tacos)

INGREDIENTS:

- 1 3 lb. chicken, stewed

- 2 large cooked potatoes

- 1 to 1 1/2 cups longhorn or cheddar cheese, grated

- Ass Kickin'™ Roasted Green Chile & Tequila Salsa or 2 (4oz) cans salsa

- Salt and pepper to taste

- 2 to 3 dozen corn tortillas

- Oil for frying

DIRECTIONS:

Dice chicken and potatoes. Add remaining ingredients, toss to blend. Soften tortillas in hot oil (Ass Kickin'™ Olive Oil is a great choice), drain. Place 1 tbsp. of chicken mixture in each tortilla, roll and fasten with a toothpick. (Taquitos may be frozen at this point).

To cook, either freshly made or frozen, heat 1/2 to 1 inch oil in pan. Add taquitos to hot oil and cook until lightly browned and crisp. Serve with guacamole on a bed of shredded lettuce and individual servings of Ass Kickin'™ Salsa.

CHICKEN TAMALE PIE

INGREDIENTS:

- 1 3 lb. whole chicken

- 2 cups corn meal

- 4 1/2 cups chicken broth

- 2 onions, chopped

- 2 cloves garlic, minced

- 2 tbsp. chile powder

- 1 can ripe olives

- 1 large can tomatoes - mashed or
  Ass Kickin'™ Whiskey Peppercorn Salsa

- 1 tsp. salt

- 1 tbsp. oil

DIRECTIONS:

Stew chicken for 1 1/2 to 2 hours until well done. Remove from broth and bone chicken and cut in pieces. Cook cornmeal in broth. Fry onion and garlic until tender and add tomatoes and chile powder. Combine corn meal, onion mixture, chicken and olives and pour into greased casserole. Bake 30 to 45 minutes in 375° oven.
Top with Ass Kickin'™ Whiskey Peppercorn Salsa or tomatoes.

ASS KICKIN'

CHILE GRILLED CATFISH

INGREDIENTS:

• 4 to 6 catfish filets, skinned and boned

• Marinade:
  2   fresh jalapeño or habañero peppers, minced
  3   fresh serranos, minced
  1/2 medium onion, chopped
  2   cloves garlic, finely minced (If using Ass Kickin'™ Garlic - you can use the habañeros on the bottom for really "HOT" catfish)
  1/2 cup oil
  1/2 cup fresh lime juice
  2   tbsp. fresh cilantro, chopped

DIRECTIONS:

Place marinade ingredients in food processor and process until well mixed using on and off pulses. Place catfish filets in glass baking dish, pour on marinade and cover. Refrigerate for 30 minutes, turn filets and marinate 30 minutes more (no longer).

Grill filets over hot coals for 2 to 4 minutes per side depending on thickness. Serve with Ass Kickin'™ Peach Rum Salsa.

CHILE TUNA SALAD

INGREDIENTS:

- 1 (7 oz.) can water packed tuna, drained and flaked

- 1 (4 oz.) can chopped green chile

- 1/2 sweet onion, chopped

- 1/4 cup green olives, chopped

- 1/2 cup celery, chopped

- 2 cups cooked elbow macaroni

- 1/4 cup mayonnaise

- 1 avocado, sliced lengthwise

- Lemon wedges

- Ass Kickin'™ Horseradish Hot Sauce to taste

DIRECTIONS:

Combine all ingredients, refrigerate 2 hours to blend flavors. Serve salad on lettuce leaf and garnish with avocado slices and lemon wedges. Top with Ass Kickin' Horseradish Hot Sauce.

CLEAR GAZPACHO

INGREDIENTS:

- 6 tomatoes, peeled and chopped

- 1 (4 oz.) can chopped green chile

- 2 1/2 quarts chicken broth

- 1 tbsp. wine vinegar

- 1 tsp. oregano

- 1 1/2 tbsp. olive oil (use Ass Kickin'™ Olive Oil for extra zip)

- 1 avocado, sliced

- Salt to taste

- Condiments: Green onion, chopped
  Salted almonds
  Cilantro
  Avocado, diced and sprinkled with lime
  or lemon juice to preserve color
  Limes, quartered

DIRECTIONS:

Mix tomatoes, broth, green chile, vinegar, oregano, olive oil and salt in large (3 quart) bowl. Chill. Add avocado just before serving. Offer condiments (for the soup) according to personal preference.

EASY BARBECUED CHICKEN

INGREDIENTS:

• 1 3 to 4 lb. chicken, cut up

• 1 bottle Ass Kickin'™ Teriyaki Sauce

DIRECTIONS:

Grill chicken over medium hot coals for 40 to 50 minutes basting with Ass Kickin'™ Teriyaki Sauce the last 10 minutes of cooking. Place bottle on the table for some extra kick!

EASY TORTILLA SOUP

INGREDIENTS:

- 1 medium onion, chopped

- 1 tbsp. oil

- 1 (4 oz.) can chopped green chile

- 4 cups chicken broth

- 1 cup cooked chicken, shredded

- 1 tomato, diced

- 2 tsp. ground red chile powder

- 1 tbsp. fresh lime juice

- 1/4 cup chopped cilantro

- Lime slices for garnish

- 6 corn tortillas, cut in 1/4 inch strips and fried in hot oil (try Ass Kickin'™ Olive Oil) until crisp or use Ass Kickin'™ Tortilla Chips

DIRECTIONS:

Saute onion and chile in hot oil in a large sauce pan until onion is limp. Add broth and chicken and simmer for 20 minutes. Add tomato and cook 5 minutes more. Stir in lime juice. Ladle into bowls and top with tortilla strips or chips. Garnish with cilantro to taste.

ENSALADA MEXICANA

INGREDIENTS:

• 1 lb. lean ground beef

• 3 tbsp. Ass Kickin'™ Popcorn Seasoning

• 4 (15 oz) cans of pinto beans, drained

• Lettuce shredded

• 1 tomato diced

• One bunch green onions, chopped including some of the tops

• Ripe olives, diced

• Cheddar or longhorn cheese, grated

• Sour cream

• Ass Kickin'™ Salsa

• Ass Kickin'™ Corn chips or regular corn tortilla chips

DIRECTIONS:

Crumble beef in 2 quart casserole, cover with waxed paper and microwave on high for 5 minutes, stirring once. Drain. Add Ass Kickin'™ Popcorn Seasoning and pinto beans. Cover and microwave mixture on medium high (70%) for 5 minutes.

Place Ass Kickin'™ Corn Chips on plate and crush. Top with meat mixture. Pass cheese, lettuce, tomato, onion, olives, sour cream, and salsa. Or tear lettuce in bite size pieces in a large salad bowl. Add meat mixture and crushed tortilla chips and toss. Top with cheese, onion and tomato.

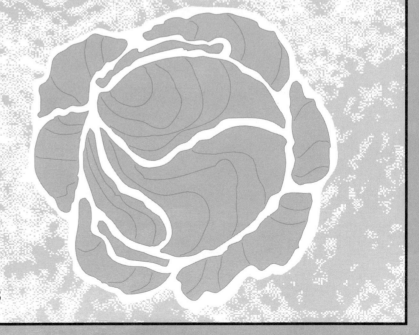

FETTUCCINE WITH PEPPER SAUCE

INGREDIENTS:

- 1 tbsp. red chile flakes (Ass Kickin'™ Original Hot Sauce works great in this recipe)

- 2 sweet red peppers, seeds removed and cut in strips

- 4 tbsp. oil

- 3 cloves Ass Kickin'™ or fresh garlic, minced

- 1 large tomato, peeled and chopped

- 1 tsp. oregano

- 1/2 tsp. basil

- 1/4 cup wine vinegar

- 4 oz. canned sliced ripe olives

- 1 lb. cooked fettuccine

- Parmesan cheese, grated

DIRECTIONS:

Saute onion and garlic in oil until soft. Add the tomato, pepper strips, oregano, basil, and crushed red pepper saute for 5 more minutes. Add vinegar and olives and heat through. Toss the sauce with fettuccine and top with grated parmesan cheese.

84

FIESTA SALAD

INGREDIENTS:

- **1 lb spiral pasta, cooked and drained**

- **1 cup Italian Salad Dressing**

- **1 (13oz) jar Ass Kickin' Salsa with Pinto Beans**

- **1 (4oz) can sliced olives**

- **1 (15oz) can whole kernel corn**

- **1 (15 oz) can kidney beans**

- **1(15 oz) can garbanzo beans**

- **1 envelope taco seasoning mix**

DIRECTIONS:

Put pasta and drained olives, corn, kidney and garbanzo beans in a large bowl and stir. Mix salad dressing, Ass Kickin' Salsa and taco seasoning together and pour over pasta mix. Toss well until all pasta and vegetables are covered with dressing. Chill and serve with Ass Kickin' Corn Chips or regular yellow corn chips.

ASS KICKIN'

GAZPACHO

INGREDIENTS:

- 1 large can (32 oz.) tomato juice

- 3 beef bouillon cubes

- 2 tomatoes, chopped

- 1 medium cucumber, diced

- 1 bell pepper, chopped

- 1/2 onion, chopped

- 1 (4oz.) can chopped green chile

- 3 tbsp. oil

- 1 tbsp. worcestershire sauce

- 1 tsp. Ass Kickin'™ Cajun Hot Sauce

- Salt to taste

- Herbed croutons

DIRECTIONS:

Heat tomato juice and bouillon to boiling. Remove from heat and cool slightly. Add remaining ingredients reserving 1/4 to 1/3 of each to be served later as accompaniments. Chill at least 3 hours and serve.

GREEN CHILE MEATLOAF

INGREDIENTS:

- 2 lbs. lean ground beef

- 2 slices cubed bread or 2 cups bread crumbs

- 1 egg

- 1 onion, diced

- 1 can diced green chile

- 1/2 cup milk

- 3-6 dashes Ass Kickin'™ Original Hot Sauce or substitute one of your favorite hot sauces

DIRECTIONS:

Combine all ingredients, form into loaf shape and place on rack in baking dish. Bake in 350º oven for 1 and 1/4 hours.

GREEN CHILE SOUP

INGREDIENTS:

- 1 onion, chopped

- 6 tbsp. unsalted butter

- 3 (4 oz.) cans green chiles, chopped

- 2 (28 oz.) cans plum tomatoes, drained

- 12 oz. cream cheese

- 2 cans chicken broth

- 3 cups half and half or 2 cups milk

- 2 1/2 tbsp. lemon juice

- Ass Kickin'™ Popcorn Seasoning to taste

DIRECTIONS:

Saute onions in butter until soft. Add green chile and tomatoes and cook 8 to 10 minutes until liquid is reduced. Stir in cream cheese until melted, but do not boil. Add remaining ingredients and sprinkle each serving with a dash of Ass Kickin'™ Popcorn Seasoning. Serve warm or at room temperature. Serves 12-16.

GREEN CHILE STEW

INGREDIENTS:

• 2 lbs. round steak, cubed

• 2 cloves Ass Kickin'™ Garlic,
  or fresh garlic cloves minced

• 1 large onion, diced

• 1 to 2 tsp. dried oregano

• 1 to 2 (4oz.) cans diced green chile

• 4 quarts water

DIRECTIONS:

Lightly brown round steak in a very small amount of oil.
Add water, onions, green chile and Ass Kickin'™ Garlic and
bring to a boil, skimming off foam. Reduce heat to a simmer
and cook 1 1/2 to 2 hours or until tender. Serve with flour
tortillas or cheese crisps.

For a heartier stew, add diced potatoes and carrots. May be
used as a topping for bean burritos.

GREEN ENCHILADAS WITH CHICKEN

INGREDIENTS:

• **Tomatillo Sauce (pg. 163)**

• **4 cups cooked turkey or chicken, shredded**

• **3 cups monterey jack cheese, grated**

• **1 (7 oz.) can chopped green chile**

• **2 tsp. oregano**

• **Salt to taste**

• **1 dozen corn tortillas**

• **Oil for frying or you can always used Ass Kickin'™ Olive Oil**

• **Sour cream**

DIRECTIONS:

Mix chicken or turkey, 2 cups of cheese, chiles, oregano, and salt. Set aside.

Fry tortillas in hot oil, turning once, until limp. Drain.

Spoon 1/2 cup of chicken mixture down center of each tortilla. Roll tortilla around filling and place seam side down in 9 x 13" baking dish (may be refrigerated at this point). Cover with foil and bake in 350° oven for 20 minutes (30 minutes if refrigerated). Uncover and top with remaining cheese and continue baking until cheese is melted.

Meanwhile heat Tomatillo Sauce. Spoon sauce on plate and place enchiladas on top. Use sour cream and cilantro leaves for garnish.

ASS KICKIN'

GREEN CHILE QUICHE IN HERB CRUST

INGREDIENTS:

• **Herb crust**
> **Dough for 9 inch pie shell**
> **1 clove garlic, minced**
> **1 tsp. parsley**
> **1 tsp. cumin**

• **Filling**
> **2 tbsp. butter**
> **1 (8 oz.) package cream cheese, crumbled**
> **1/2 cup ricotta cheese**
> **4 eggs, beaten**
> **1/4 cup cream or half and half**
> **1/2 cup Ass Kickin'™ Roasted Green Chile & Tequila salsa**
> **1/4 cup romano cheese, grated**

DIRECTIONS:

Add the garlic, parsley, and cumin powder to the pie crust dough and blend well. Form the dough into a pie pan. Prick with a fork and bake partially in a 450° oven for 8 to 10 minutes. Cool.

Dot the cooled pie shell with butter. Next add the crumbled cream cheese and ricotta cheese. Beat the eggs and cream. Pour the mixture into the pie shell. Top with the Ass Kickin'™ Green Chile & Tequila Salsa and grated cheese. Bake for 45 minutes in a 350° oven or until brown and set. Serves 6 to 8 as an appetizer.

91

GREEN BEAN CHILE

INGREDIENTS:

• 1 lb. lean ground beef

• 1 small onion, chopped

• 1 clove Ass Kickin'™ Garlic minced

• 2 cans french cut green beans, drained

• 1 can whole or diced tomatoes

• 1 (8 oz.) can tomato sauce

• 1 (4 oz.) can chopped green chile

• Ass Kickin'™ Hot Sauce, to taste

• Salt and pepper to taste

DIRECTIONS:

Brown ground beef, onion, and garlic in a skillet. Drain. In a large saucepan, combine green beans, tomatoes, tomato sauce, green chile, and seasoning. Add meat and simmer for 30 to 45 minutes stirring occasionally. Serve with cheese crisps or Ass Kickin'™ Tortilla Chips.

ASS KICKIN'™

GREEN CHILE BURROS

INGREDIENTS:

• 4 lbs. lean boiling beef or pork, well cooked

• 1 tsp. red chile powder

• 2 (4 oz.) cans green chile, chopped

• 1/2 to 1 tsp. oregano

• 1 large onion, chopped

• 2 cloves garlic, minced (Ass Kickin'™ Garlic will really heat it up)

• 2 cups beef broth

• 4 tbsp. flour

• Salt and pepper to taste

• 4 tbsp. Ass Kickin'™ Olive Oil or regular olive oil

• Large flour tortillas

DIRECTIONS:

Cut cooked beef into 1/2 inch cubes or shred. Brown in oil over low heat. Add flour, chile powder, green chile, onion, garlic, oregano and beef broth. Mixture should be fairly thick. Add more flour if needed. Heat tortillas on griddle or wrap in foil and heat 10 minutes in oven. Fill tortilla with 3 to 4 tbsp. of meat mixture. Fold over sides and roll. Enjoy as is or cover with enchilada sauce and shredded cheese.

Variation: RED CHILE BURROS

Using above recipe, substitute 1 tbsp. red chile powder for green chiles.

Variation: CHIMICHANGAS

Deep fry burros in hot oil until golden brown. Drain. Top with shredded lettuce, grated cheese, guacamole, sour cream, and Ass Kickin'™ Salsa.

ASS KICKIN'™

GREEN CHILE CHICKEN ENCHILADAS

INGREDIENTS:

- 1 2 to 3 lb. chicken

- 1 large onion, chopped

- 2 cloves Ass Kickin'™ Garlic or fresh garlic, chopped

- Salt to taste

- 2 (4oz.) cans chopped green chile

- 1 tbsp. red pepper flakes, optional

- Flour to thicken

- 12 corn tortillas

- 1/2 lb. grated longhorn or cheddar cheese

- 1 onion, chopped

- Shredded lettuce

- Diced tomato

- Sour cream

DIRECTIONS:

Cook chicken in water with onion, garlic, and salt. Remove chicken from stock, cool and remove meat from bones. Cool stock and refrigerate. Degrease. Return chicken to 4 cups of stock, add chiles. Thicken stock with 1/4 cup flour mixed with 1/4 cup water.

To assemble enchiladas: Lightly fry tortillas in oil 10 - 15 seconds, drain on absorbent paper. On each plate, place tortilla, grated cheese, chopped onion, and 1/4 cup chicken mixture. Repeat layers to desired serving size.

Top with shredded lettuce, tomato, and sour cream.

Each tortilla may be filled with cheese and onion, then rolled and placed in 9 x 12" baking dish. Cover with sauce and bake in 350° oven for 30 minutes or until bubbly hot.

GRILLED JALAPEÑO CHEESE BURGERS

INGREDIENTS:

• 2 lbs. lean ground beef

• Salt and pepper to taste

• 1 (4 oz.) package cream cheese, regular or fat-free

• 2 tbsp. onion, finely chopped

• 2 tbsp. jalapeño or habañero peppers, finely chopped. Grab the habañeros lurking in the bottom of your Ass Kickin'™ garlic jar for *"Real Heat"*.

DIRECTIONS:

Shape ground beef into 16 thin patties. Combine cream cheese, onion, and jalapeños or habañeros and spread on 8 of the patties. Place remaining patties on top and press edges to seal in cheese mixture. Grill to desired doneness. Serve with your favorite condiments.

"HOT" ROAST

INGREDIENTS:

- 21/2 to 3 lb beef roast

- 1/4 cup Ass Kickin" Popcorn Seasoning or another dry seasoning rub

- 4-6 potatoes (cut into 1/4 wedges)

- 1 medium onion sliced

- 1/2 cup beef broth

DIRECTIONS:

Place roast in the center of a 9x11" roasting pan. Rub generously with Ass Kickin' Popcorn Seasoning until completely covered. Place potatoes and onions evenly around roast and sprinkle with additional seasoning. Pour beef broth into pan and bake 1 1/2 to 2 hours in a 325° oven. Turn potatoes every 1/2 hour.

MEXICAN DIP SANDWICH

INGREDIENTS:

- 2 lbs. round steak, thinly sliced (easier to slice if partially frozen)

- 2 yellow peppers chopped very small or habañero peppers for "*real*" heat

- 2 (4oz.) cans chopped green chile

- 1 large can tomato sauce

- 1 or 2 large onions, chopped

- 1/2 cup vinegar

- Ass Kickin'™ Olive Oil for browning meat

- Salt and pepper to taste

- Flour tortillas

DIRECTIONS:

Saute peppers and onions in part of the Ass Kickin'™ Oil. Add meat and brown. Then add remaining ingredients and simmer slowly at least 1 hour (longer is better).

Warm tortillas in foil in the oven. Place meat filling in tortilla and provide bowl for dipping in the left over sauce.

MEXICAN LASAGNA

INGREDIENTS:

- 1 1/2 lbs. lean ground round

- 1 medium onion, chopped

- 1 (16 oz.) can tomatoes without juice

- 1 (10 oz.) can enchilada sauce or 1 cup red chile sauce (pg. 161)

- 1 can ripe olives, drained and sliced

- 1/4 tsp. each garlic powder and pepper

- 1 tsp. salt

- 1/4 cup Ass Kickin'™ Olive Oil or regular olive oil

- 6 to 8 corn tortillas

- 1 cup small curd cottage cheese

- 1 egg

- 1/2 lb. each monterey jack and cheddar cheese, thinly sliced or shredded

- Shredded lettuce

- 1 jar Ass Kickin'™ Whiskey Peppercorn Salsa or one of your other favorites

DIRECTIONS:

Brown meat and onion in large frying pan. Drain. Add enchilada sauce, tomatoes, black olives, salt, pepper and garlic powder. Bring to boil, reduce heat and simmer uncovered 20 minutes. Meanwhile soften tortillas in hot Ass Kickin'™ Olive Oil a few seconds on each side. Drain on absorbent paper and cut in half. Blend egg and cottage cheese together in small bowl. In a 9 x 12" baking dish or a 3 quart casserole spread 1/3 of meat sauce on bottom. Top with half of the Jack cheese and half of the cottage cheese, then 1/2 of the tortilla halves. Repeat layering, ending with final 1/3 of the meat sauce. Top with cheddar cheese. Bake, uncovered, in a 350⁰ oven for 25 to 30 minutes. Let stand for 5 minutes before serving. Top with shredded lettuce and Ass Kickin'™ Whiskey Peppercorn Salsa.

MEXICAN CHICKEN CASSEROLE

INGREDIENTS:

- 6 cooked chicken breasts, diced
- 1 can cream of mushroom soup
- 1 can diced tomatoes
- 1 can cream of chicken soup
- 1/2 cup chicken broth
- 1/4 tsp. garlic powder
- 1 bag Ass Kickin'™ Corn Chips or regular corn tortilla chips
- 1/3 lb. grated longhorn or cheddar cheese
- Black olives, optional

DIRECTIONS:

Mix together soups, tomatoes, broth and garlic powder. Line 9 x 12" baking pan with Ass Kickin'™ Corn Chips. Top with diced chicken. Pour soup mixture over chicken and cover with another layer of chips. Sprinkle on cheese and optional black olives. Heat in 350° oven 30 minutes or until heated through and cheese is melted.

ASS KICKIN'

MEXICAN MEAT LOAF

INGREDIENTS:

- 4 tbsp. butter or margarine
- 3/4 cup onion, chopped
- 1/2 cup celery and bell pepper, chopped
- 1/4 cup green onions, chopped
- 1 tbsp. Ass Kickin' Hot Sauce™
- 1 tbsp. worcestershire
- 1 tbsp. salt
- 1 tsp. cayenne
- 1 tsp. black pepper
- 1 tsp. cumin
- 1/2 cup evaporated milk
- 1/2 cup Ass Kickin'™ Ketchup or regular ketchup
- 2 lbs. lean ground beef
- 2 eggs
- 1 cup bread crumbs

DIRECTIONS:

Melt butter in a sauce pan and saute the vegetables along with the spices for 5 minutes or until vegetables are tender. Add milk and ketchup and cook 2 minutes. Remove from heat and cool. Mix together the beef, eggs, and bread crumbs. Add vegetable mixture thoroughly.
Shape the mixture into a 12 x 6 x 1 1/2" loaf. Bake in 350° oven for 25 minutes, raise oven temperature to 400° and continue baking for 35 minutes. Serve as is or with this savory sauce.

SAUCE INGREDIENTS:

- 3/4 cup onion, chopped
- 1/2 cup bell pepper, chopped
- 1/4 cup celery, chopped
- 1/4 cup jalapeño peppers, seeded and chopped
- 1 clove garlic, minced
- 1/4 cup oil (Ass Kickin'™ Olive Oil works great)
- 1/4 cup flour
- 3/4 tsp. cayenne
- 1/2 tsp. black pepper
- 3 cups beef stock

SAUCE DIRECTIONS:

Saute onion, bell pepper, celery, jalapenos, and garlic in the oil until tender. Add flour and seasonings and stir until well mixed. Slowly add the beef stock, stirring constantly over medium heat, until mixture reaches a gravy-like consistency. Serve as a sauce for meat loaf.

MEXICAN STUFFED SHELLS

INGREDIENTS:

- **12 jumbo pasta shells**
- **1 lb ground beef**
- **1 cup Ass Kickin' Original Hot Sauce or use picante sauce**
- **1 (8oz) can tomato sauce**
- **1/2 cup chicken broth**
- **1 (4 oz) can chopped green chilies**
- **1/4 tsp. ground cumin**
- **1/8 tsp. chili powder**
- **1 1/2 cups shredded monterey jack cheese**

DIRECTIONS:

Cook pasta according to package instructions. Drain well and set aside. Cook ground beef in skillet, break up into small pieces while cooking, drain and set aside. In a mixing bowl combine Ass Kickin' Hot Sauce, tomato sauce, chicken broth, cumin and chile powder, blend well.
Add 1/2 cup sauce mixture, green chilies and 1/2 cup cheese to beef and mix well. Spread approximately 1/2 of mixture that is left on the bottom of a 9x12" greased baking dish. Stuff pasta shells with beef mixture. Place shells in baking dish and pour remaining sauce over top. Pre-heat oven to 350°, cover shells with foil and bake for 30 minutes. Uncover and top with remaining cheese. Return shells to oven and bake an additional 5 to 10 minutes, or until cheese is melted.

MEXICAN PIE

INGREDIENTS:

- 1 lb ground beef

- 1/2 onion chopped

- 1 clove garlic minced

- 1 envelope taco seasoning mix

- 1 (4oz) can diced green chiles

- 1 1/4 cup milk

- 3/4 cup Bisquick

- 3 eggs

- 1 tbsp. Ass Kickin' Roasted Garlic Hot Sauce

- 1 cup shredded monterey jack cheese

DIRECTIONS:

Brown ground beef, add onion and saute with beef. Blend in seasoning mix and place in a 10 inch pie plate. Place cheese and chilies over top of beef. Mix milk, Bisquick, eggs and Ass Kickin' Hot Sauce and pour over cheese. Bake at 350° for 30-40 minutes.

MICROWAVE TORTILLA SOUP

INGREDIENTS:

- 2 tbsp. oil

- 1 medium onion, chopped

- 1 clove garlic, minced

- 1/2 tsp. cumin

- 4 cups chicken broth

- 1 (4 oz.) can chopped green chile

- Salt to taste

- Chopped fresh cilantro

- 6 corn tortillas, cut in strips and fried crisp or Ass Kickin'™ Corn Chips

DIRECTIONS:

Combine oil, onion, garlic and cumin in 2 quart glass bowl. Cover with wax paper and microwave on high for 2 minutes. Add broth and green chile to mixture, cover and continue to cook on high for 10 minutes, stirring after 5 minutes. Season to taste. Serve soup with tortilla strips or Ass Kickin'™ Corn Chips and garnish with cilantro.

NAVAJO TACOS

INGREDIENTS:

- 1 lb. lean ground beef

- 1 large onion, chopped

- 1 to 2 cloves fresh garlic, chopped or - use Ass
  Kickin'™ Garlic, it's great!

- 3 cups cooked pinto beans

- 1/2 to 2/3 cup Red Chile Sauce (pg. 161)

- Indian Fry Bread (pg. 29)

- Shredded lettuce

- Grated longhorn or cheddar cheese

- Chopped onion

- Diced tomato

DIRECTIONS:

Saute onion and Ass Kickin'™ Garlic, add ground beef and brown. Drain. Add Red Chile Sauce to taste. Stir in pinto beans and heat through.

Prepare Indian Fry Bread according to recipe. Top each piece of fry bread with beef and bean mixture.

Pass lettuce, tomato, onion, Ass Kickin'™ Salsa and cheese to top each taco. Serves 4.

PEANUT CHICKEN

INGREDIENTS:

- 2 whole chicken breasts, boned and skinned

- 1 egg white

- 1 tbsp. cornstarch (coating)

- 1 tsp. sherry

- 1 tsp. sesame oil, optional

- 1/2 tsp. sugar

- 1/3 cup cold water

- 2 tbsp. Ass Kickin'™ Teriyaki Sauce

- 1 tsp. cornstarch (to thicken)

- 3 tbsp. oil

- 1 tsp. crushed red pepper

- 4 cloves Ass Kickin'™ Garlic, minced

- 2 tsp. grated ginger

- 1/2 cup Ass Kickin'™ Peanuts

- 8 oz. Chinese pea pods

- 4 cups cooked rice

DIRECTIONS:

Cut chicken into 1 inch pieces. In a bowl, combine egg white, 1 tbsp. cornstarch, sherry, sesame oil, sugar, and chicken pieces, tossing to coat chicken with mixture. Set aside. In a small bowl combine cold water, Ass Kickin'™ Teriyaki Sauce and 1 tsp. cornstarch. Set aside.

Heat oil in wok or large skillet over high heat. Stir-fry red pepper, Ass Kickin'™ Garlic, and ginger for 15 to 30 seconds - do not burn. Add chicken pieces and stir-fry for one minute. Stir in water, teriyaki and cornstarch mixture and cook while stirring for 2 minutes or until thickened and bubbly.
Stir in Ass Kickin'™ Peanuts and pea pods and heat through. Spoon over hot cooked rice. Serves 4.

POLLO CON VINO

(CHICKEN WITH WINE)

INGREDIENTS:

- 1 3 to 4 lb. stewing chicken

- 6 tbsp. oil (or make it hot with Ass Kickin'™ Olive Oil)

- 1 medium can tomatoes

- 1 tsp. oregano

- 1/2 tsp. sage

- 1 clove garlic minced

- 1 tsp. parsley flakes

- 2 tsp. chile powder

- 1/2 cup dry white wine

DIRECTIONS:

Cut chicken into serving size pieces and brown in large skillet with oil. Remove chicken from pan and pour off excess oil. Add tomatoes, garlic, oregano, sage, parsley, chile powder, and wine to pan and simmer 5 minutes. Add chicken pieces and cover. Simmer gently 1 1/2 to 2 hours. Serve over rice or pasta. Serves 6.

ASS KICKIN'™

PECHUGAS DE POLLO CON ROJAS

(Chicken breast and chiles)

INGREDIENTS:

- 6 chicken breasts, skinned, boned and cut into strips

- 1 large onion, thinly sliced

- 4 (4 oz.) cans whole green chiles, cut into strips

- 2 tbsp. butter or margarine

- 1/2 cup milk

- 2 cups sour cream

- 1 cup cheddar cheese, grated

DIRECTIONS:

Saute chicken in butter. Drain on paper towel and set aside.
Saute onions and half the chiles until onion is soft.
In blender or processor combine rest of chile, milk, and sour cream; blend until smooth.
In a deep casserole, layer 1/2 chicken, 1/2 chile/onion mixture, and 1/2 the sauce. Repeat.
Top with grated cheese.
Bake at 350° until hot, about 1/2 hour.
Do not overcook.
Serve over rice if desired or alone with tortillas.
Serves 6.

ASS KICKIN'

POSOLE

INGREDIENTS:

- 1-3 lb. pork loin

- 1 package frozen posole or 2 large cans white hominy

- 1 large onion, chopped

- 2 tsp. oregano

- 2 large cloves Ass Kickin'™ Garlic, or fresh minced

- 2 tbsp. salt

- 4 (4oz.) cans chopped green chile or 8-10 fresh, roasted chiles, peeled and stems removed

DIRECTIONS:

Boil pork loin until tender. Cool and cut into medium size cubes. Reserve and degrease broth.

If using frozen posole, thaw and rinse well with cold water. Place in large pot, cover with 2 quarts of water, simmering at least 1 hour or until the posole kernels burst. Drain and add to broth. If using canned hominy, drain and wash. Combine hominy with reserved broth, pork cubes, onion, oregano, garlic and salt. Simmer, covered for 3 hours, adding more water if needed. Add chiles during the final hour.

VARIATIONS:

Add a 16 oz. can of tomatoes during the final hour of cooking.

Add 3 to 4 tbsp. Red Chile Sauce (pg.161)

Serve Posole in soup bowls with flour tortillas, Ass Kickin'™ Corn Chips or regular tortilla chips.

Tantalizing accompaniments: shredded lettuce, diced radish, chopped green onion, fresh cilantro and additional Red Chile Sauce.

PEACH RUM CHICKEN

INGREDIENTS:

- 2 lbs. boneless, skinless chicken breasts

- 1/4 cup flour

- 1 tsp. salt

- 1/4 tsp. pepper

- 2 tbsp. butter

- 1 tbsp. vegetable oil

- 1 (13oz) jar Ass Kickin'™ Peach Rum Salsa

- 1/2 cup sour cream

- 1 cup shredded cheddar cheese

DIRECTIONS:

Combine flour, salt and pepper. Dredge chicken in flour mixture. Heat butter and oil in fry pan. Add chicken and brown 5 minutes on each side. Remove from fry pan and place in a greased 9x13" baking dish. Combine Ass Kickin'™ Peach Rum Salsa and sour cream. Pour over chicken. Bake at 350° for 30 minutes or until center of chicken is no longer pink. Top with cheese and return to oven for an additional 5 minutes or until cheese melts.

109

RED CHILE CON CARNE

INGREDIENTS:

- 1 lb. lean boiled beef or leftover roast cut in cubes

- 2 cups hot beef broth

- 3 tbsp. flour

- 3 tbsp. oil or try some "heat" with Ass Kickin'™ Olive Oil

- 1 tbsp. chile powder

- 1 tsp. salt

- 1/4 tsp. pepper

- 1 onion, chopped

- 1 clove Ass Kickin'™ Garlic minced

- 1 can tomato puree

DIRECTIONS:

Heat oil in large skillet and brown meat cubes. Add flour, onion, garlic, chile, tomato puree and seasonings, stir and simmer for 5 minutes. Add broth to mixture. Cover and simmer over low heat for 45 minutes.

RED OR GREEN CHILE PASTA WITH CHEESE SAUCE

In heavy saucepan melt butter, stir in heavy cream, Ass Kickin'™ Hot Sauce, salt and pepper to taste and bring just to boiling. Pour over pasta, sprinkle on parmesan and toss well to coat. Serve with chicken, fish, beef, or alone with crusty French bread and a salad.

INGREDIENTS:

• Red Chile Pasta or Green Chile Pasta

• Cheese Sauce
  2 tbsp. butter
  1/2 cup heavy cream
  1/2 cup parmesan cheese, grated
  Ass Kickin'™ Hot Sauce or salt and
  pepper to taste

DIRECTIONS:

Cook fresh pasta in boiling water for 2 to 3 minutes until just tender. Dried pasta will take 7 to 10 minutes. Drain. Place in large shallow serving bowl.

RED PEPPER STEAKS WITH SALSA FRESCA

INGREDIENTS:

• 4 boneless steaks, cut 1 to 1 1/2 inches thick

• Marinade:
>2 tsp. dried red chile powder
>1 tsp. dried red pepper flakes
>1/2 cup wine vinegar
>2 tbsp. fresh lime juice
>1 tbsp. Ass Kickin'™ Fajita Marinade or
>   1 tbsp. soy sauce
>Zest from one lime
>1/4 cup olive oil or vegetable oil
>2 cloves garlic minced, use Ass Kickin'™
>   garlic as a "Hot choice"
>Salt and fresh ground pepper to taste

• Salsa Fresca:
>3 to 4 ripe tomatoes, diced

• Lime slices

DIRECTIONS:

Combine marinade ingredients in sealable plastic bag. Reserve 1/4 cup to baste meat while cooking. Add meat to marinade, place in refrigerator 8 hours or overnight, turning occasionally.

Remove steaks and discard marinade. Grill steaks over medium coals to doneness desired - 7 to 8 minutes per side for rare, 9 to 10 for medium. Turn meat only once and baste with the reserved marinade.

RED SNAPPER VERACRUZ

INGREDIENTS:

• 1 onion, chopped

• 4 shallots, minced

• 2 cloves garlic, minced

• 1 carrot, grated

• 1 tbsp. oil (Heat it up using Ass Kickin'™ Olive Oil)

• 1 (14 oz.) can stewed tomatoes, drained and chopped

• 1 (4 oz.) can chopped green chiles

• 3 tbsp. lemon juice

• 2 tbsp. fresh cilantro or 2 tsp. dried cilantro

• Cayenne pepper to taste

• Salt and pepper to taste

• 2 lbs. red snapper

DIRECTIONS:

Saute onion, shallots, garlic, and carrots in Ass Kickin'™ Olive Oil until the onion is soft. Add tomatoes, chiles, lemon juice, and cilantro. Simmer for 5 minutes. Salt and pepper to taste.

Place snapper in 9 x 12" baking dish. Pour sauce over the top and bake in 350° oven for 20 minutes or until fish flakes easily and is opaque. Broil briefly to brown the vegetables. Serves 6 to 8.

ROASTED GREEN CHILES

INGREDIENTS:

- **Green chiles**
  Choose fully matured green chiles that have not turned red.

DIRECTIONS:

Wash green chiles in sink or large tub. Puncture pods with fork and roast on a charcoal grill until they begin to blister.

When skin is evenly blistered and puffed away from the pulp, place pods in a large bowl and cover with a damp cloth to steam.

Chiles may be pealed and used immediately or frozen in plastic bags for future use.

SHRIMP KABOBS

INGREDIENTS:

Sauce

- 1/4 cup butter, melted
- 1 tsp. dried thyme
- 1/2 tsp. pepper
- 1/4 tsp. cayenne pepper
- 2 tbsp. Ass Kickin'™ Ketchup
- 1 tsp. Worcestershire sauce
- 1/2 tsp. fresh garlic minced

   OR USE

- 1/2 cup Ass Kickin'™ Fajita Marinade

Kabobs

- 1 pound (20-25) fresh shrimp peeled and deveined
- 1 large sweet onion cut into 1" wide slices
- 1 red or green bell pepper cut into 1x1" pieces
- 12 6" wooden skewers soaked in water

DIRECTIONS:

Blend all sauce ingredients. Marinate shrimp, onions and peppers for a minimum of 1 hour, or marinate using Ass Kickin'™ Fajita Marinade.

Prepare grill, either charcoal or gas. On each skewer place shrimp, onion and pepper alternating until skewer is full. Place on grill and cook until shrimp is pink (8-10 minutes) turning frequently. Serve with warm tortillas and a tossed salad.

115

SOPA DE QUESO

(MEXICAN CHEESE SOUP)

INGREDIENTS:

• 5 cups hot beef broth

• 2 tsp. ground red chile

• 1 onion, chopped

• 1 large can tomatoes

• 1/2 lb. longhorn or cheddar cheese, grated

• 2 tbsp. oil

• 1 tbsp. flour

• 1/2 tsp. oregano

DIRECTIONS:

Heat oil in large saucepan. Add flour, tomatoes, onion, and chile. Stir. Add beef broth and simmer for 15 minutes. Add grated cheese and continue cooking for 1 hour.

SONORAN ENCHILADAS

INGREDIENTS:

• 12-14 dried New Mexican red chiles

• 2 lbs lean pork, cubed

• 2 cloves Ass Kickin'™ Garlic or fresh garlic, minced

• Flour

• Salt

• Corn tortillas

• 1 onion, diced

• 1 lb. grated longhorn or cheddar cheese

• Shredded lettuce

• Diced tomatoes

• Fried egg, optional

• Oil (Ass Kickin'™ Olive Oil heats this up nicely)

DIRECTIONS:

Roast chiles on a cookie sheet 6 inches from broiler; it takes about 1 minute. Watch carefully as they burn easily. (Discard any that burn; they are bitter). When cool, remove stem and seeds, then place in blender with at least 1 cup of water. Blend until pureed.

Saute garlic and add cubed pork that has been dredged in flour and brown in oil. Remove all but about 2 tbsp. of oil from pan, add 4 tbsp. of flour and brown. Add 3 cups of water and cook until thickened. Reduce heat, add chile puree and simmer until pork is tender (30 minutes). More water may be added if sauce is too thick. Salt to taste.

Fry tortillas in hot oil 10 to 15 seconds, turning once. Drain.

To assemble enchiladas, place tortilla on oven proof plate, top with diced onion, grated cheese, and a large tablespoon of sauce. Repeat layers (2 or 3), ending with sauce. Top with cheese and place in oven to keep warm; prepare additional servings. Top with shredded lettuce, diced tomatoes, and egg.

SOUTHWESTERN PORK CHOPS

INGREDIENTS:

- 6 pork chops (approx 1/4" thick)

- 4 poblano chiles

- 3 corn tortillas (cut into 1" squares)

- 1 small bunch fresh cilantro (remove long stems)

- 1/4 cup water

- 2 tbsp. fresh garlic chopped

- 2 tbsp. Olive Oil (Use Ass Kickin' for heat)

- Salt & pepper to taste

DIRECTIONS:

Roast and peel poblano chiles and set aside. In a large skillet, brown pork chops in olive oil and remove. Drain oil from pan. Place roasted chiles, garlic, water, corn tortillas and cilantro into a blender and blend until smooth. Pour sauce into skillet and bring to a boil. Reduce heat and add pork chops to skillet. Simmer for approximately 20 minutes. (If sauce becomes too thick add additional water 1 tbsp. at a time until sauce reaches desired consistency.) Serve over rice or braised cabbage.

STUFFED BELL PEPPERS

INGREDIENTS:

- 1 lb lean ground beef

- 1 egg

- 1 large onion chopped

- 2 cloves garlic minced

- 4 green bell peppers

- 1/2 cup Ass Kickin'™ Ketchup or regular ketchup

- 1 cup seasoned bread crumbs

- 1/2 tsp. salt

- 1/2 tsp. pepper

- 1/4 tsp. cayenne pepper

DIRECTIONS:

Cut top off of bell peppers and remove seeds and stem, wash and set aside. Combine all ingredients except bell peppers into a bowl and mix well. Stuff peppers with beef mixture and place in an 8x8" baking dish. Bake at 325° for 45 minutes.

SPICY BAKED CHICKEN

INGREDIENTS:

- 6 chicken breasts, boned and skinned

- 2 eggs

- 1 clove garlic, minced

- Ass Kickin'™ Roasted Garlic Hot Sauce or taco sauce

- 1 1/2 cup fine bread crumbs

- 2 tsp. chile powder

- 2 tsp. ground cumin

- 1/4 cup melted butter or margarine

- Shredded lettuce

- Avocado, sliced

- Sour cream

- Green onions, chopped

- Cherry tomatoes, halved

DIRECTIONS:

Rinse chicken, pat dry and set aside. In a small bowl, beat eggs, garlic, and 1/4 cup Ass Kickin'™ Roasted Garlic Hot Sauce or taco sauce. In another bowl, mix together bread crumbs, chile powder, and cumin. Dip chicken in egg mixture and then in crumbs. Place chicken pieces in a 9 x 13" baking dish. Pour melted butter over chicken and bake in 375° oven for 30 to 35 minutes or until meat in thickest part is no longer pink.

Serve chicken on a bed of lettuce, topped with a dollop of sour cream. Garnish with avocado slices, green onion, and cherry tomatoes. Serves 6.

SPICY ROAST TURKEY

INGREDIENTS:

- 1 10 to 12 lb. turkey

- Spice rub
    - 1/4 cup red chile powder
    - 1 tsp. garlic powder
    - 1 tsp. ground cumin

DIRECTIONS:

With cold tap water clean the turkey, then dry. Rub the turkey with the spice mixture, lifting the skin over the breast area to rub spices into breast meat along with the inside cavity. Reserve any remaining spices and add to 2 tbsp. of oil to baste the turkey while roasting.

Prepare barbecue with about 60 to 70 briquettes. When coals are white hot, divide them into two rows on the outer edge of the grill. Add 10 briquettes to each side so the temperature in the grill remains constant. Place a drip pan (4 by 12 inches), made from a double thick, heavy duty piece of foil between the two strips of coals. Place unstuffed turkey, breast side down, on the grill at least 6 inches above the coals and over the drip pan. Close the grill lid, making sure the air vents are open, and cook for one half the cooking time recommended for the weight of the turkey, (generally 20 minutes per pound).

Turn the turkey so the breast is up, baste with oil and spices and continue cooking and basting periodically until meat thermometer reads 185° in the thickest part of the thigh, being sure not to touch the bone. (You may need to add more briquettes to maintain temperature.)

If you want to make gravy, carefully remove the drip pan from the grill. Put drippings in a sauce pan and follow your best gravy recipe.

Serve with Green Chile Cornbread Dressing (pg. 178).

SWORDFISH

INGREDIENTS:

• 4 swordfish fillets

• 4 to 6 tbsp. Ass Kickin' Olive Oil

• 1/2 cup sliced green onions (including tops)

• 1/2 cup chopped fresh parsley

• Seasoning salt to taste

• 1 large tomato diced

• 1 fresh lemon cut into wedges

• 1 fresh lime cut into wedges

DIRECTIONS:

Place swordfish in a single layer in a baking dish, coat each piece well with Ass Kickin' Olive Oil. Top with green onions and bake uncovered in a 350° oven until fish is just slightly translucent, (10-20 minutes). Sprinkle with seasoning salt, place on serving dish and top with parsley and tomatoes.

TAMALES

INGREDIENTS:

- 10 lbs. prepared tamale masa* (see pg. 124)

- 5 lbs. pork

- 5 lbs. beef

- 6 cloves garlic, minced (use Ass Kickin'™ Garlic for real taste)

- 4 tbsp. chile flakes

- 2 jars Santa Cruz Chili or Baca's Hot Red Chili

- 1 large can Los Palmas Red Chili Sauce

- 2 tbsp. oregano

- 1 tbsp. cilantro

- 1 tbsp. garlic powder

- 1 tsp. ground cumin

- 2 packages dried corn husks

- Green olives, optional

DIRECTIONS:

Boil meat with garlic and chili flakes for 3 hours. Remove meat from broth (reserve), cool, and shred. Add chili sauces, oregano, cilantro, garlic powder, and cumin, stirring to combine. If mixture is too dry, add reserved broth a little at a time to moisten mixture. (Mixture should not be soupy, just fairly "wet.")

To prepare tamales:
1. Soak corn husks in hot water to soften. Remove from water, drain, and cover with a damp cloth until ready to use.

2. Remove masa from refrigerator; if too dry add some reserved broth and incorporate. Place a tablespoon of masa on a corn husk and spread with the back of spoon to cover husk in a rectangular shape.

3. Place a rounded tablespoon of meat mixture in center of masa (top with one olive if desired) and fold both sides of corn husks over mixture enclosing meat. Fold up pointed end of husk to make an envelope. Double tamales may be made if the husks are wide. If that is the case, use as much masa as you need to cover the husk, leaving the pointed end uncovered. Add meat to two sides and roll loosely to the middle. Fold up end.

4. Put a rack in the bottom of a large kettle. Elevate so 2 to 3 inches of water can be added with the rack sitting above the water level. If there are any leftover corn husks they may be placed on top of the rack.

(Continued)

Stand tamales, open end up, on rack and steam for 1 hour or until masa pulls away from husk.

5. Remove husks and serve. Or cool and freeze in sealable plastic freezer bags.

6. To reheat frozen tamales, place on rack and steam until hot through, about 1/2 to 3/4 of an hour, or microwave about 3 minutes, checking after 2 minutes. Do not over-cook; tamales dry out and get tough.

Makes 80 to 100 tamales depending on size. The process can be tedious if done alone, but is plenty of fun if done with a group.

* If prepared masa is not available, follow these instructions:

INGREDIENTS:

• **2 10 lb. bags of masa harina**

• **3 tbsp. salt**

• **2 lbs. shortening or lard**

• **10 cups beef stock**

DIRECTIONS:

Combine 8 cups stock with shortening, breaking up shortening with hands. Add masa harina and salt and continue mixing with hands, kneading the dough until it is light and fluffy, adding more stock if mixture is too dry.

TACOS

INGREDIENTS:

- 1 lb. ground beef

- 1 potato, diced

- 1/2 onion, diced

- 1/4 cup Ass Kickin'™ Hot Sauce

- 1 dozen corn tortillas or prepared taco shells

- Grated cheese

- Shredded lettuce

- Diced tomatoes

DIRECTIONS:

Fry potato in a small amount of oil until brown. Remove from pan and brown ground meat and onion. Drain excess grease. Add potatoes and Ass Kickin'™ Hot Sauce, stirring to coat. Keep warm. Fry tortillas in hot oil and drain. Fill taco shells with meat mixture and top with cheese. Pass the lettuce and tomatoes and more Ass Kickin'™ Hot Sauce.

TORTILLA SOUP

INGREDIENTS:

- 1 2 to 3 lb. chicken

- 1 tbsp. olive oil

- 1 large onion, chopped

- 2 cloves garlic, minced

- 1 (15 oz.) can tomatoes

- 1 (4 oz.) can green chile or 5 to 6 fresh green chiles, roasted, peeled, seeded, and chopped

- 1 tsp. cumin

- 2 tsp. ground red chile

- 1 tsp. oregano

- 1/4 cup cilantro, chopped

- 6 corn tortillas, cut in 1/2 inch strips

- Oil for frying

DIRECTIONS:

Cover chicken with water and bring to a boil. Reduce heat and simmer for 1 to 2 hours or until tender. Skim off any foam that forms. Remove chicken, strain broth and reserve. Remove chicken from the bones, cut or tear into bite size pieces and return to 5 cups of the broth.

Saute onion and garlic in olive oil until tender. Add green chile and continue cooking for a few more minutes. Add to chicken and broth along with tomatoes (broken up and with juices), cumin, red chile powder, and oregano. Bring to a boil, reduce heat and simmer for 30 minutes. Add cilantro just before serving.

Fry tortilla strips in batches in hot oil until crisp. Drain. (Add some heat, use Ass Kickin'™ Olive Oil)

Place soup in bowl and top with tortilla strips.

TUNA LOAF

INGREDIENTS:

- 4 (6 1/2 oz) water packed tuna drained
- 3 cups fresh bread crumbs (6 slices of bread)
- 2 eggs, slightly beaten
- 2 (4oz) cans diced green chiles
- 1/4 cup chopped onion
- 3 tbsp. lemon juice
- 2 tsp. chicken bouillon
- Ass Kickin' Roasted Garlic Hot Sauce

DIRECTIONS:

Preheat oven to 350º. In a large bowl, combine all ingredients; except hot sauce and mix well. Place in a greased shallow baking dish or loaf pan. Bake 30 to 40 minutes. Let stand 10 minutes before serving. Top with Ass Kickin' Hot Sauce and serve.

SAUCES AND APPETIZERS

BEAN DIP

INGREDIENTS:

- **2 lbs. lean ground round**

- **2 onions, chopped**

- **2 cans ranch style pinto beans**

- **1 can cream of chicken soup**

- **2 (4 oz.) cans chopped green chiles**

- **2 lbs. Velveeta™ cheese, cubed**

- **Ass Kickin'™ Salsa to taste or another of your favorite salsas**

DIRECTIONS:

Brown ground round and onion in large, heavy saucepan. Drain. Add beans, green chile, soup (undiluted), cubed Velveeta, and salsa. Simmer, stirring often until the cheese melts and dip is hot. Serve warm with Ass Kickin'™ Tortilla chips.

BLACK BEAN DIP

INGREDIENTS:

• 6 slices bacon, diced, fried and drained

• 1 medium onion, chopped

• 1 tsp. Ass Kickin'™ Popcorn Seasoning

• 1 (15 oz.) can black beans, drained (reserve liquid)

• 1/4 lb. monterey jack cheese, grated

• 1/4 cup green onions, sliced (including tops)

• Sour cream

• Guacamole

• 1 Jicama, peeled and cut into sticks

• Ass Kickin'™ Corn Chips

DIRECTIONS:

Saute onions in small amount of oil until tender. Mash black beans adding reserved liquid (as needed to make beans "creamy"), bacon, Ass Kickin'™ Popcorn Seasoning and onions. Spread to an 8" round on a large platter. Top with guacamole, sour cream, cheese, and green onion. Serve with jicama sticks and Ass Kickin'™ Corn Chips.

CALIFORNIA CHILE DIP

INGREDIENTS:

- 1 pint sour cream

- 1 envelope dry onion soup mix

- 1 (4oz.) can green chiles, chopped

- 1/2 tsp. garlic salt

- 1/4 tsp. Ass Kickin'™ Hot Sauce

DIRECTIONS:

Mix together all ingredients and chill for at least 2 hours to blend flavors.

CHEESE CRISP WITH RED CHILE SAUCE

INGREDIENTS:

• 1 cup Red Chile Sauce (pg. 161)

• 4 oz. each monterey jack and cheddar cheese, grated

• 8 corn tortillas

• Butter or margarine

DIRECTIONS:

Melt 2 tablespoons butter in large frying pan over medium heat. Place tortilla in pan. When slightly softened place cheese on one half folding the other half over on top. Repeat until pan is filled, adding more butter as needed. When tortilla is lightly brown, turn over and continue cooking. Place in warm oven until all tortillas are cooked.

Arrange on plate and spoon Red Chile Sauce over the top.

CHILE CHEESE LOG

INGREDIENTS:

- 5 or 6 fresh green chiles, roasted, peeled, seeded and chopped or 1 (4 oz.) can chopped green chile

- 1 (8 oz.) package cream cheese, softened

- 1/2 lb. sharp cheddar cheese, grated

- 1 clove garlic, mashed with a little salt to make a paste

- 1/2 cup chopped pecans

- Red chile powder

DIRECTIONS:

Mix garlic paste with cream cheese. Add grated cheese, green chile, and pecans. Form into a log, wrap in wax paper and refrigerate for 1 hour. Remove log from wax paper and roll in red chile powder. Rewrap and refrigerate until ready to serve. Great with an assortment of crackers and Ass Kickin'™ Tortilla Chips.

CHILE CON QUESO

INGREDIENTS:

- 1 (2lb.) package Velveeta cheese

- 1 (13oz.) jar Ass Kickin'™ Salsa

- 1 (4oz.) can diced green chile

- 1/2 medium onion, chopped

DIRECTIONS:

Cube Velveeta cheese, place in microwave safe casserole. Cook on high power for 5 minutes, stirring once. Remove from oven and stir in 1/2 jar of Ass Kickin'™ Salsa, green chile, and onion. Return to microwave and cook on medium power for 3 to 4 minutes, stirring once. May require more cooking time to thoroughly melt the cheese. If mixture is too thick, add more Ass Kickin'™ Salsa. Serve with tortilla chips.

CRANBERRY SALSA

INGREDIENTS:

- 4 tsp. grated orange peel

- 2 large oranges

- 2 cups cranberries, sorted

- 1/4 cup onion, minced

- 1/4 cup salad oil

- 1 tbsp. fresh cilantro, minced

- 1 tbsp. fresh ginger, minced

- 1 small fresh jalapeno or habañero pepper, stemmed, seeded, and minced - (Grab the habañero from the bottom of your Ass Kickin'™ Garlic jar!)

- Salt to taste

DIRECTIONS:

Remove remaining peel and white membrane from oranges. Remove seeds and chop oranges and drain in a colander. Whirl cranberries in food processor until chopped. Add to orange zest, drained oranges, onion, oil, cilantro, ginger, and jalapeño or habañero. Stir to blend and season with salt. Cover and refrigerate until ready to serve. Makes 3 cups.

CHICKEN WINGS

INGREDIENTS:

- **25 chicken wings**

- **1 (12 oz) bottle Ass Kickin™' Chicken Wing Sauce; or use sauce recipe below**

- **Salt & pepper to taste**

CHICKEN WING SAUCE RECIPE:

INGREDIENTS:

- **1 dip stick unsalted**

- **Bottled Hot Sauce**

DIRECTIONS:

Melt butter in a sauce pan and add as much hot sauce as you like. Normal store bought hot sauce heat is as follows; 2 tbsp. for mild, 4 tbsp. for medium and 6 to 8 tbsp. for hot.

DIRECTIONS:

Cut chicken wings into 3 pieces discarding the tips. Place wings on a greased cookie sheet or a cookie sheet that is covered with foil. Pre-heat oven to 350° and bake 30 to 35 minutes.
Pour 1/2 bottle Ass Kickin'™ Chicken Wing Sauce in a bowl, place cooked wings inside and toss until all wings are well coated.   Serve with bleu cheese dressing and celery sticks, and extra chicken wing sauce for dipping.

CHILE CUCUMBER DIP

INGREDIENTS:

- 2 large cucumbers, peeled and minced

- 1 tsp. salt

- 1 (8 oz.) package cream cheese at room temperature

- 1/4 cup sour cream

- 1/4 cup chopped green chile

- 3 to 4 dashes Ass Kickin'™ Hot Sauce

DIRECTIONS:

Put the cucumber in a colander and sprinkle with salt. Set the colander in a dish and refrigerate for an hour to release liquid. Cream the cheese and sour cream together until blended. Add well drained cucumber, green chile and Ass Kickin'™ Hot Sauce. Taste, salting if necessary. Serve with raw vegetables or crackers.

CHILE PESTO AND CREAM CHEESE

INGREDIENTS:

• 1 cup Green Chile Pesto (pg. 150)

• 12 oz. cream cheese, at room temperature

• 1 tbsp. milk

• Fresh cilantro

DIRECTIONS:

In a small bowl, blend cream cheese and milk until smooth. Line a small bowl or mold with plastic wrap and alternate layers of cream cheese and pesto, starting and ending with cream cheese. Wrap plastic wrap over the top and refrigerate in the bowl at least 8 hours. Remove the cheese from the bowl and unwrap on serving plate. Garnish with fresh cilantro leaves. Serve with a baguette or crackers.

CHILE POTATO SKINS

INGREDIENTS:

- **5 large or 10 small potatoes**

- **Butter or margarine, softened**

- **Longhorn or cheddar cheese, grated**

- **1 (13 oz.) jar Ass Kickin'™ Whiskey Peppercorn Salsa or another favorite prepared salsa**

- **Sour cream**

- **Green onions, chopped**

DIRECTIONS:

Scrub potatoes, pierce with a fork, and bake in a 400° oven about 1 hour or until done. Cool potatoes until you can handle them. Cut potatoes in half lengthwise and scoop out the flesh, leaving 1/8 to 1/4 inch thick shell. (May be refrigerated until ready to use.) Lightly butter inside of potato skins and place on baking sheet.

Bake in 500° oven until crisp, about 10 minutes. Remove from oven and divide grated cheese between shells and return to oven to melt cheese. Serves 6 to 10.

Top with sour cream and sprinkle with chopped green onions. For extra zip, add the famous Ass Kickin'™ Whiskey Peppercorn Salsa.

CHILE CARIBE

(Base for red chile sauce)

INGREDIENTS:

• 10 to 12 chile pods (seeded and stemmed)

• 1 tsp. salt

• 1 clove Ass Kickin'™ Garlic

• 1/4 tsp. oregano

• 2 1/2 cups water

DIRECTIONS:

Rinse out chile pods. Place all ingredients in blender and blend to a smooth paste.

DOUBLE "T" SALSA

INGREDIENTS:

• 1 lb. ripe Roma tomatoes, washed and cored

• 3 medium tomatillos, husked, rinsed and cored

• 1/2 cup fresh cilantro, chopped

• 1 clove Ass Kickin'™ Garlic, minced

• 1/4 cup lime juice

• 2 Jalapeño or habañero peppers, stemmed, seeded, and minced

• Salt to taste

DIRECTIONS:

Place tomatoes and tomatillos in food processor and process using off and on pulses to finely chop mixture. Do not puree. Transfer to a bowl and add rest of ingredients mixing well. Refrigerate covered until ready to use. Serve with Ass Kickin'™ Corn Chips.

FIESTA DIP

INGREDIENTS:

- 1 (16 oz.) can refried beans

- 1 (4 oz.) can green chiles, chopped

- 1 (16 oz.) carton sour cream

- 1 tomato, chopped

- 1 (16 oz.) container frozen avocado dip

- 1/2 cup red onion, chopped

- 1 (4 oz.) can ripe olives, chopped

- 1 cup cheddar cheese, grated

- **Ass Kickin'™ Corn Chips**

DIRECTIONS:

Layer the ingredients in the order listed on a 12" plate.
Place the plate on a large platter. Surround with chips.

5 LAYER DIP

INGREDIENTS:

- 1 (12 oz) jar Ass Kickin'™ Black Bean Dip

- 1 (8oz) container sour cream

- 1 envelope taco seasoning

- 3 green onions chopped with stems

- 1 medium tomato diced

- 1 cup shredded cheddar cheese

- 1 (10 to 12 oz) bag corn chips

DIRECTIONS:

Spread Ass Kickin' Black Bean Dip on a 12 to 14" plate. Mix taco seasoning with sour cream and spread over top of bean dip. Layer green onions, tomato & cheddar cheese over top. Place chips in a bowl and serve next to dip plate.

GARLIC SPREAD

INGREDIENTS:

- 1 (8oz) package cream cheese, softened

- 1/2 cup butter or margarine softened

- 2 tbsp. chopped parsley

- 2 cloves Ass Kickin'™ Garlic, minced

- 2 tbsp. chopped onion

DIRECTIONS:

Combine cream cheese and butter and mix until well blended. Add remaining ingredients and blend well. Cover and place in refrigerator for at least one hour. Serve with crackers, fresh vegetables or slices of warm french bread.

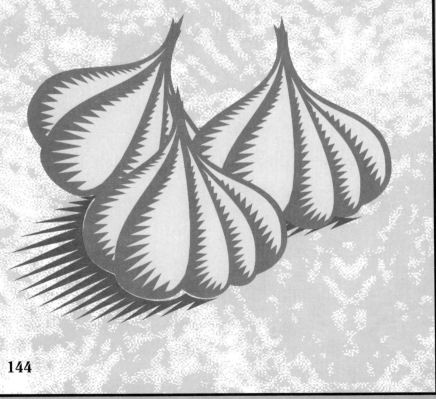

GARDEN DIP

INGREDIENTS:

- 1 (8 oz.) package cream cheese, softened

- 1/2 cup mayonnaise

- 1/2 cup small curd cottage cheese

- 1/2 tsp. garlic salt

- 1 (4 oz.) can green chile, chopped

- 2 tsp. fresh chives, finely chopped

- Ass Kickin'™ Popcorn Seasoning or salt to taste

DIRECTIONS:

Mix the cream cheese, mayonnaise, cottage cheese, garlic salt, and Ass Kickin'™ Popcorn Seasoning or salt in a blender. Stir in chives and green chiles. Serve with potato or Ass Kickin'™ Tortilla Chips.

GOAT CHEESE TORTE

INGREDIENTS:

• **8 oz. cream cheese**

• **8 oz. goat cheese**

• **3 sticks butter, softened**

• **1 cup Green Chile Pesto (pg. 150)**

• **1 cup sun-dried tomatoes, drained and minced**

DIRECTIONS:

Beat cheese and butter until well blended and fluffy. Line a small springform pan or any decorative bowl with plastic wrap. Fill with 1/3 of the cheese mixture, followed by 1/2 of the pesto and repeat layers ending with cheese mixture. Chill 1 hour. Unmold and top with diced sun-dried tomatoes. Serve at room temperature with sliced baguettes or crackers.

GUACAMOLE

INGREDIENTS:

- 2 ripe avocados

- 2 green onions, minced

- 2 tomatoes, chopped fine

- 2 to 4 green chiles, chopped

- Juice of 1/2 lemon

- Salt and pepper to taste

Optional

- 1/2 jar Ass Kickin'™ Roasted Green Chile & Tequila Salsa

DIRECTIONS:

Mash avocados. Add remaining ingredients and mix well. Can be made ahead and refrigerated. Cover with plastic wrap to seal.

GREEN CHILE TORTILLA PINWHEELS

INGREDIENTS:

- 4 flour tortillas

- 1 (8 oz.) package cream cheese

- 1 (4 oz.) can chopped green chile, drained

- 1 tsp. Ass Kickin'™ Popcorn Seasoning or salt to taste

DIRECTIONS:

Soften cream cheese, then blend in chile and red chile powder. If too stiff, add a teaspoon of milk until spreading consistency. Spread mixture on each tortilla and roll up jelly roll style. Wrap in plastic and refrigerate. To serve, cut in 1/2" slices.

GREEN CHILE CHEESE

INGREDIENTS:

- 1/2 lb sharp cheddar cheese, grated

- 8 to 10 fresh, roasted green chiles, peeled, seeded and chopped or 2 (4 oz.) can chopped green chile, drained

- 6 green onions, minced with part of the tops

- 2 cloves garlic, finely minced - (use Ass Kickin'™ Garlic for *real* flavor and heat)

- 1 small jar pimentos, drained and slivered

- Mayonnaise

DIRECTIONS:

Mix all ingredients with enough mayonnaise to make a spreading consistency. Refrigerate overnight so flavors blend. Serve as a spread for crackers, baguettes, or bagels.

149

GREEN CHILE PESTO

INGREDIENTS:

• 2 cups fresh green chile, roasted, peeled, and chopped

• 1 cup freshly grated parmesan cheese

• 3 cloves garlic, finely minced

• 1/2 cup cilantro, chopped

• 1 tsp. salt

• 2/3 cup pine nuts

• 1 cup virgin olive oil (Ass Kickin'™ Olive Oil is extra virgin and hot!)

DIRECTIONS:

Put all ingredients in food processor except the olive oil. Start the machine and through the feed tube add the oil in a steady stream. Refrigerate so the flavors blend. Store in the refrigerator for up to 4 days or freeze for 2 months.

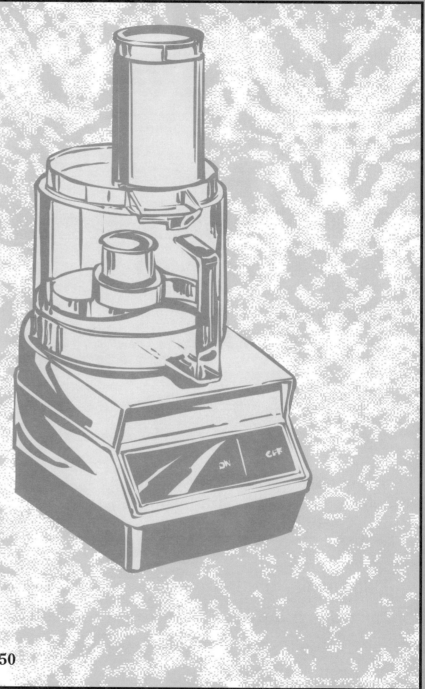

GREEN PEPPER JELLY

INGREDIENTS:

- 4 1/2 cups sugar

- 1 1/2 cups white vinegar

- 1 1/2 cups red pepper, minced

- 1 cup green pepper, minced

- 2 small dried chile peppers, seeded and crumbled

- 3/4 tsp. salt

- 1 (6 oz.) bottle liquid pectin

DIRECTIONS:

Combine sugar, vinegar, peppers, and salt in a large sauce pan. Boil, stirring until sugar dissolves. Stir in the liquid pectin and cook over medium-high heat until 222° on a candy thermometer.
Seal with melted paraffin in hot, sterilized jars.
Serve with cream cheese and crackers.

JELLY

HOT & SOUR PICKLES

INGREDIENTS:

• 2 lbs. pickling cucumbers

• 3 cups cider vinegar

• 1 cup water

• 1/4 cup dry mustard

• 1/4 cup salt

• 1/4 cup sugar

• 1 tsp. crushed chiltipins or dried habañero peppers

• 1 small sweet onion, quartered (optional)

DIRECTIONS:

Wash cucumbers and pack with onion into 2 (1 quart) canning jars. Mix remaining ingredients until dissolved. Pour over cucumbers to fill jars and cap. Pickles do not have to be processed nor do they have to be refrigerated. Store pickles for 48 hours before serving.

ASS KICKIN'™

HOT PICKLED CARROTS

INGREDIENTS:

• 4 pounds large carrots, peeled

• Water

• 1/4 cup olive oil

• 1 large onion, chopped

• 4 cloves of garlic, halved

• 2 cups distilled vinegar

• 1 bay leaf

• 1 tsp. each dry oregano and dry thyme leaves

• 1 tsp. whole black pepper

• 1/2 tsp. salt

• 2 habañeros
  Habañeros from the bottom of the Ass Kickin'™
  Pickled Garlic work great

DIRECTIONS:

Cut carrots diagonally into 1/4 inch slices. Bring 4 quarts water to a boil in a 6 to 8 quart pan over high heat; add carrots, return to a boil and cook, covered just until carrots still have a little crispness (bite to test), 1 to 2 minutes. Drain, then immerse carrots in cold water; when carrots are cold, drain. Wipe pan dry and place over medium high heat. Add oil, onion, and garlic and cook, stirring often, until onion is soft. Stir in vinegar, bay leaf, oregano, thyme, black pepper, salt, habañeros and their liquid, and carrots. Bring to a boil, then remove from heat. Using a slotted spoon, place carrots in a 3 to 4 quart jar or bowl. Pour vinegar mixture over the carrots and cool. Cover and refrigerate, stirring occasionally, for 24 hours before serving. Carrots will keep for 3 to 4 weeks. Makes about 3 quarts.

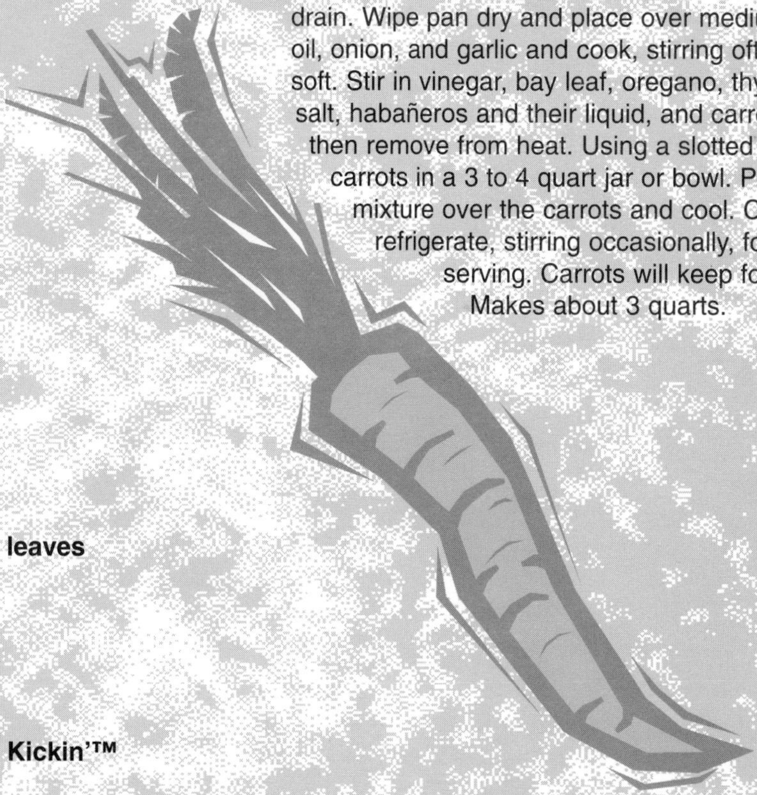

HABANERO PICKLED EGGS

DIRECTIONS:

Put all ingredients in a gallon jar; fill the jar the top with boiling water. Cover the jar with plastic wrap and screw on the lid and leave at room temperature. Mix daily by turning jar over. Refrigerate after 5 days.

INGREDIENTS:

- 3 dozen small eggs, hard-cooked and peeled

- 1 quart cider vinegar

- 1 (12 oz) jar pickled habaneros

- 2 large onions sliced

- 1/4 cup salt

- Boiling water

JICAMA & FRUIT PLATE

INGREDIENTS:

- 1 medium jicama, peeled and cut in strips

- Choose from any or all of the following fruits:
    - Honeydew
    - Cantaloupe
    - Watermelon
    - Papaya
    - Mango
    - Orange slices
    - Kiwi
    - Green Apple

- 1 tsp. salt

- 1 tbsp. chile powder

DIRECTIONS:

Prepare fruit: peel, seed, core. Cut in bite size pieces and arrange on large plate. Mix salt and chile powder and sprinkle over fruit. A refreshing appetizer or light dessert.

MANGO PINEAPPLE SALSA

DIRECTIONS:

Combine all ingredients in bowl. Refrigerate until ready to use. Keeps about 4 days in refrigerator. Excellent served with beef, pork, or chicken.

INGREDIENTS:

• 1 ripe mango, diced

• 1/4 fresh pineapple, diced

• 1/2 cup purple onion, chopped

• 1 cup yellow or red bell pepper, chopped

• 1 serrano chile, finely chopped

• Juice of one lime

• 1/4 cup fresh cilantro, finely chopped

MINI COCKTAIL MEATBALLS

DIRECTIONS:

Preheat oven to 375°.
In a mixing bowl combine all ingredients and mix well. Shape into 1" meatballs. Place meatballs in a shallow baking pan and bake 18-20 minutes.

Serve with toothpicks and additional Ass Kickin' Hot Sauce for dipping.

INGREDIENTS:

- **1 envelope onion soup mix**

- **1 lb lean ground beef**

- **1/2 cup plain bread crumbs**

- **1/4 cup cooking sherry or water**

- **2 eggs, beaten**

- **2 tbsp. Ass Kickin' Roasted Garlic Hot Sauce**

MUSHROOM RELLENOS

INGREDIENTS:

- 25 medium sized fresh mushrooms

- 6 green chiles

- 6 tbsp. sour cream

- 1/4 tsp. garlic salt

- 1/4 tsp. salt

- 1 tbsp. Ass Kickin'™ Roasted Garlic Hot Sauce or dash of pepper

- 5 tbsp. butter or margarine

- 5 tbsp. dry white wine

DIRECTIONS:

Remove the mushroom stems and reserve. Chop the stems and the green chiles into small pieces. Add the sour cream, garlic salt, salt, Ass Kickin'™ Hot Sauce, 2 tablespoons wine, and 3 tablespoons butter. Mix thoroughly into a smooth paste.

Stuff the mixture into the mushroom caps. Pour the remaining wine into a 9 x 12" baking dish and dot with the remaining butter. Add the stuffed mush-rooms to the pan, cover, and bake in preheated 325° oven for 25 minutes.

NACHOS

INGREDIENTS:

- 1 (10 oz) bag Ass Kickin' Corn Chips OR

- 1 (10 oz) bag yellow corn tortilla chips

- 1 1/2 cup grated cheddar cheese

- 1 (4 oz) can diced green chilies

- 1/4 cup chopped green onions including stems

- 1/2 cup canned black beans drained

- 1/2 cup diced fresh tomatoes

- 1 (13 oz) jar Ass Kickin'™ Salsa or another of your favorites

DIRECTIONS:

Place corn chips in a 9x13" baking pan, top with all ingredients evenly, ending with the cheese. Bake or broil until all cheese is melted . Serve warm with side dishes of salsa for dipping.

PICANTE DIP

INGREDIENTS:

- 1 (16 oz.) can tomatoes

- 1 onion, chopped

- 6 to 8 green chiles, chopped

- 2 (8 oz.) packages of cream cheese, softened

- 1/4 tsp. ground red chile

DIRECTIONS:

Simmer tomatoes and onions about 20 minutes. Cool mixture until it is only warm. Add remaining ingredients and mash to incorporate the cheese to desired consistency for a dip. Serve with Ass Kickin'™ Corn Chips.

RED CHILE SAUCE

(for dipping, tacos, tostadas, taquitos)

INGREDIENTS:

- 4 tbsp. red chile powder

- 3 tbsp. Ass Kickin'™ Olive Oil

- 2 tbsp. flour

- 2 cups beef stock

- 2 cups tomato sauce

- 1/2 tsp. oregano

- Pinch of coriander

- Salt to taste

DIRECTIONS:

Heat oil, add flour, salt, spices, garlic, and tomato sauce. Heat beef stock with chile powder and add slowly, stirring constantly to sauce mixture. Simmer for 15 minutes. Keeps well in refrigerator for up to a week.

RED CHILE OIL

INGREDIENTS:

- **1 cup dried red chiles - piquin, cayenne, jalapeño or habañero**

- **2 cups vegetable oil**

DIRECTIONS:

Heat oil in a saucepan to 350°. Remove it from the heat and add the chiles, and let the oil stand to cool. Cover the pan and let stand for 12 to 24 hours (the longer, the hotter). Strain the oil and bottle.

USES:

Great for stir-fry, popcorn, spicy salad dressings, or as an all purpose oil to add zip to any recipe.

SALSA VERDE

(Green Chile Sauce)

INGREDIENTS:

- 2 (4oz.) cans chopped green chile or 10-12 fresh green chiles, roasted, peeled, and chopped

- 1 medium onion, chopped

- 1 clove garlic, minced

- 1 tbsp. oil

- 1 tbsp. flour

- 1 tomato, peeled and chopped

- 1 cup chicken broth

- 1/4 tsp. ground cumin

DIRECTIONS:

Saute onion and garlic (use Ass Kickin'™ Garlic for some heat) in oil until soft. Stir in flour, blending well, and cook a few minutes. Add remaining ingredients, bring to a boil, reduce the heat and simmer until sauce has thickened.

SAUCE FOR CHILE PASTA

INGREDIENTS:

• 1 to 2 cloves Ass Kickin'™ Garlic or fresh, chopped

• 1 medium onion, chopped

• 1 large tomato, chopped or 1 small can tomatoes, drained

• Ass Kickin'™ Olive oil

• Salt and pepper to taste

• Fresh grated parmesan cheese

DIRECTIONS:

Saute garlic and onions in olive oil. Add tomato and seasonings and heat through. Pour over chile flavored pasta and sprinkle with parmesan cheese.

SALSA FRESCA

INGREDIENTS:

- 6 large tomatoes, chopped

- 1 large onion, chopped

- 4 to 6 anaheim chilis, chopped

- 6 cloves garlic

- 1/4 to 1/2 cup chopped cilantro

- 1 to 2 tbsp. Ass Kickin'™ Hot Sauce

- 1 1/2 tsp. salt

- 1 tsp. seasoned pepper

- 1/2 tsp. olive oil

- 1 tsp. oregano

- 1 tbsp. wine vinegar

DIRECTIONS:

Blend all ingredients together. Add more hot sauce to taste.

SHRIMP COCKTAIL

INGREDIENTS:

- 1 1/2 lb medium-size shrimp, shelled, deveined and cooked

- 1/2 cup Ass Kickin'™ Ketchup

- 1 tsp. grated lime peel

- 1/4 cup lime juice

- 1/4 cup dry white wine

- 1/4 tsp. Ass Kickin'™ Hot Sauce

- Shredded lettuce

DIRECTIONS:

Mix together, Ass Kickin'™ Ketchup, lime peel, lime juice, wine, and hot sauce. Add shrimp, mix well to coat, and refrigerate, covered. Serve on a bed of lettuce in chilled cocktail or sherbet glasses. Serves 6 to 8.

SOUTHWEST PHYLLO PILLOWS

INGREDIENTS:

• **Phyllo dough**

• **Butter, melted**

• **Filling**
    1 lb. cheddar cheese, grated
    1 lb. monterey jack cheese, grated
    1/2 cup Ass Kickin'™ Green Chile & Tequila
    Salsa or another one of your favorites

DIRECTIONS:

Mix all filling ingredients together.

Remove three sheets of phyllo dough at a time. Brush the top of each sheet with butter and stack. Keep other sheets covered with a dish towel so they don't dry out. Cut each stack into 3 inch sheets. Add 1 tsp. of filling to one end of each strip and fold as you would a flag - in triangles. Continue until filling is used. Brush tops with butter. Pillows may be frozen at this point. Bake at 350° for 10 minutes on a cookie sheet. If baking frozen, they may take a few minutes longer. Watch closely.

STUFFED JALAPENOS

INGREDIENTS:

• 1 large can jalapeño peppers, drained
  (reserve liquid)

• 1 (8oz.) package cream cheese, softened

• 1/2 tsp. garlic salt

• 2 tbsp. finely minced green onion

DIRECTIONS:

Mix cheese, onion, and garlic salt together. If the mixture is
too stiff, thin with a small amount of milk until a smooth,
creamy texture is achieved.

Pat jalapeños dry, cut in half lengthwise, and remove seeds.
Put cheese mixture in pastry bag fitted with a large star tip
or in a wax paper cone with 1/4 inch cut off the end. Pipe
the cheese mixture into center of the chiles. Sprinkle with
Ass Kickin'™ Popcorn Seasoning, chile powder or paprika
and refrigerate until ready to serve.

TOMATILLO SALSA

INGREDIENTS:

- 1 1/4 lbs. fresh tomatillos, husks removed, or 1 can of tomatillos

- 1/3 cup cilantro, chopped

- 2 cloves Ass Kickin'™ Garlic, minced

- 1 jalapeño chopped or habañero pepper

- 3/4 cup chicken broth

- 1/3 cup fresh lime juice

DIRECTIONS:

Rinse tomatillos, and roast in 500° oven until lightly singed - about 15 minutes. Cool. Place remaining ingredients in food processor and blend until well mixed. Cover and refrigerate until ready to use. Keeps in refrigerator for 3 to 4 days.

SIDE DISHES

CALABACITAS

(squash)

INGREDIENTS:

- 1 tbsp. butter or Ass Kickin'™ Olive Oil

- 4 medium zucchini squash or 6 yellow summer squash

- 1 medium onion, chopped

- 1 clove garlic - Make it "oh so hot" with Ass Kickin'™ Garlic

- 1 can whole corn, drained

- 1 small can chopped green chile, or 4 fresh roasted green chiles seeded and diced

- 1/2 cup longhorn or Jack cheese, grated

- Salt and pepper to taste

DIRECTIONS:

Saute in skillet, squash, onion, and garlic in oil. Add green chile and corn. Cover and cook 10 minutes over medium heat. Lower heat, add cheese and cook until cheese melts about 2 or 3 minutes. Serves 6-8.

CARNE ADOBADA

(pork in hot chile sauce)

INGREDIENTS:

- 3 cups Red Chile Sauce (pg. 161) or 18 to 24 dried red New Mexico chiles

- 3 cups water

- 4 cloves garlic, chopped (try Ass Kickin'™ Garlic)

- 1 tbsp. oregano

- 3 lbs. lean pork, cubed

- Salt to taste

DIRECTIONS:

Rinse chiles, cover with water and bring to a boil. Reduce heat and simmer for 10 to 15 minutes until softened. Place chiles, garlic and oregano in blender along with chile liquid and puree until smooth. Strain to remove skins and seeds.

Marinate pork in Red Chile Sauce 3 to 4 hours or overnight in the refrigerator. Cover and bake in 300° oven for 2 to 3 hours until meat is very tender and starts to fall apart. Uncover for final 30 minutes to reduce the sauce. Serve wrapped in flour tortillas or as an entree.

172

CHILE AVOCADO GRAPEFRUIT SALAD

INGREDIENTS:

• 2 grapefruit, peeled and sectioned

• 2 ripe avocados, peeled and sliced

• Jicama, cut into match sticks, optional

• Lettuce leaves

• Dressing
    1/4 cup sugar
    1 tsp. salt
    1 tsp. chile powder
    1 tsp. dry mustard
    1/4 cup lemon or lime juice
    1/2 cup salad oil
    1 tsp. grated onion juice

DIRECTIONS:

Whisk the dressing ingredients together or shake well in a jar until blended. Arrange lettuce leaves on salad plates. Arrange grapefruit and avocado slices in fan. Pour on dressing just before serving. Serves 4.

CHILE RELLENO CASSEROLE

INGREDIENTS:

- 1 large can whole green chile or 16 fresh chiles, roasted and peeled

- 1 lb. monterey jack cheese, cut in strips

- 1/2 lb cheddar cheese, grated

- 5 eggs

- 1/4 cup flour

- 1/4 cup milk

- Ass Kickin'™ Popcorn Seasoning or salt and pepper to taste

DIRECTIONS:

Stuff peppers with Jack cheese and place in 9 x 12" baking dish. Cover with grated cheese. Blend eggs, milk, flour, and spices and pour over chiles. Bake in 350° oven for 30-40 minutes, or until set.

CHILE RELLENOS

INGREDIENTS:

- 8 to 10 green chiles, roasted and peeled

- cheddar or jack cheese cut into strips

- Flour for dredging

- 2 eggs, beaten

- Ass Kickin'™ Olive Oil for frying

- Garlic salt

- Tomato salsa (recipe to follow)

DIRECTIONS:

Make a slit in the side of each chile and stuff with cheese. Dredge chiles in flour and then beat eggs with garlic salt. Dip chiles in egg and fry in 1/2 inch of hot Ass Kickin'™ Olive Oil until golden brown. Drain on paper towel. Put in large casserole in a single layer, cover with tomato salsa and bake in 350° oven for 30 minutes.

TOMATO SALSA INGREDIENTS:

- 1 small can tomato sauce

- 1 can diced tomatoes or 1 can taco sauce

- 1 tbsp. chili powder

- 1 tsp. comino seeds or 1 tsp. ground cumin

- 1 tbsp. minced cilantro (Mexican parsley)

- Salt to taste

DIRECTIONS:

Combine all ingredients and pour over chiles.

CORN SALSA

INGREDIENTS:

- 4 jalapeño chiles, chopped

- 1 small red, yellow, or green bell pepper, chopped

- 1 tomato, chopped

- 1/2 cup whole kernel corn, drained

- 1/2 red onion, chopped

- 1 clove garlic, chopped

- 3 tbsp. salad or Ass Kickin'™ Olive Oil

- 1 tbsp. lime juice

- 1 tbsp. cilantro, chopped

DIRECTIONS:

Combine all ingredients in a medium sized bowl. Mix thoroughly and refrigerate for 1-2 hours. Serve with Ass Kickin'™ Corn Chips, regular corn chips or as a topping for eggs or nachos.

176

CORNBREAD

INGREDIENTS:

- 1 1/2 cups white cornmeal

- 3 tbsp. flour

- 1 tsp. salt

- 1 tsp. baking soda

- 2 cups buttermilk

- 1 egg, beaten

- 2 tbsp. melted margarine or drippings

- 2 to 4 tbsp. Ass Kickin'™ Hot Sauce

DIRECTIONS:

Combine dry ingredients. Add buttermilk, melted margarine, Ass Kickin'™ Hot Sauce and beaten egg. Preheat oven to 450° oven in which you have put a large ovenproof heavy (cast iron, preferably) skillet. Carefully remove pan from hot oven (remember the handle is very hot) and oil lightly. Pour mixture into pan and return to oven for 20 to 25 minutes.

177

GREEN CHILE CORNBREAD DRESSING

INGREDIENTS:

• 1 recipe cornbread (pg. 177) or your own favorite mix, crumbled (Ass Kickin'™ Corn Bread Mix works great)

• 10 slices stale white bread, cubed

• 1 large onion, chopped

• 8 celery ribs, chopped

• 8 to 10 fresh green chiles, roasted, peeled, and chopped or 2 (4 oz.) cans chopped green chile

• 2 to 3 tbsp. butter or margarine

• 1 egg, beaten

• 1 to 2 tbsp. rubbed sage or to taste

• 1 1/2 cups broth (turkey or chicken)

• Salt and pepper to taste

DIRECTIONS:

In a large bowl break up cornbread and combine with bread cubes. Saute the onion and celery in margarine until tender. Add onion mixture, green chile, sage, and salt and pepper to the bread mixture and mix. Add egg and broth and combine until mixture is moist. You may need to add a bit more broth if the dressing is too dry. Spray a 9 x 13" baking dish with vegetable spray and add the dressing mixture, do not pack. Bake in 350° oven for 30 to 35 minutes.

GREEN CHILE CHEESE GRITS

INGREDIENTS:

- 1 cup quick grits

- 4 cups water

- 1/2 cup butter or margarine

- 1/2 to 3/4 cup grated cheese

- 1/2 cup diced green chile

- 2 or 3 eggs

- Milk

- Garlic, lemon, seasoned salt, or Ass Kickin'™ Popcorn Seasoning to taste

DIRECTIONS:

Bring water to a boil and slowly add grits, stirring constantly. Return to boil, cover and reduce heat to simmer. Cook 3 minutes. Meanwhile beat eggs in measuring cup and fill to 1 cup measure with milk. Combine egg mixture, grits, chile, cheese and seasonings in a casserole. Cover and bake 45 minutes. Uncover and bake 15 minutes more. Serves 6-8.

GREEN CHILE CORN

INGREDIENTS:

- 2 cans creamed corn

- 1/4 cup corn meal

- 3/4 tsp. Ass Kickin'™ Popcorn Seasoning or garlic salt

- 1 tsp. baking powder

- 1/3 cup oil

- 2 beaten eggs

- 4 to 6 roasted green chiles diced, or 1 (4 oz.) can diced green chile

- 2 cups grated longhorn, cheddar, or jack cheese

DIRECTIONS:

Combine all ingredients and pour into a 2 quart greased casserole. Bake in 350° oven for 45 minutes. Serves 4-6.

GREEN CHILE POTATO BOATS

INGREDIENTS:

• 4 cups mashed potatoes

• 6 to 8 roasted, peeled green chiles

• 1/2 cup shredded longhorn, cheddar, or Jack cheese

• Ass Kickin'™ Popcorn Seasoning

DIRECTIONS:

Carefully slit green chile open and remove seeds leaving stem intact. Fill chiles with mashed potatoes and form into boats. Top with cheese and place in casserole sprayed with cooking oil. Sprinkle each with Ass Kickin'™ Popcorn Seasoning. Bake 30 minutes or until hot in a 350° oven. Serves 6-8.

GREEN PASTA

INGREDIENTS:

• 3 tbsp. chopped green chile or jalapeños

• 3 large eggs, at room temperature

• 2 tsp. olive oil or Ass Kickin'™ Olive Oil

• 2 cups flour

• 2 tbsp. water

DIRECTIONS:

Put eggs, jalapeños, and olive oil in food processor and puree. Add the flour and process until the dough forms a ball. If the mixture does not come together, add water 1 tsp. at a time until the dough forms a ball. Knead by hand on lightly floured board until the dough is soft and elastic. Divide dough into quarters. Cover portions not in use so they don't dry out. Roll dough out very thin by hand or use a pasta machine following directions.

Cut the sheets of pasta into desired widths. If not using immediately, dry the pasta completely and place in air tight bags.

Cook fresh pasta in boiling water for just a few minutes until al dente - firm to the bite. Dried pasta will take longer.

GREEN BEANS SUPREME

INGREDIENTS:

• 1 can cream of mushroom soup

• 3 cans whole green beans, drained

• 4 tbsp. milk

• 1 (4 oz.) can green chile, chopped

• 1/4 lb. sharp cheddar cheese, grated

• 1/4 tsp. garlic salt or Ass Kickin'™ Popcorn Seasoning

• 1 can french-fried onions

DIRECTIONS:

Combine all ingredients except the onion rings in a greased casserole. Stir lightly to blend well. Bake in preheated 350º oven for 25 minutes. Remove from oven and sprinkle onions on top. Return to oven and bake 10 minutes longer. Serves 8.

GRILLED ZUCCHINI

INGREDIENTS:

- 4 small zucchini

- Olive oil or heat it up with Ass Kickin'™ Olive Oil

- Chile powder

- 1 tbsp. oregano

- 2 tbsp. parmesan cheese, grated

DIRECTIONS:

Cut zucchini in half lengthwise. Brush with oil and place cut side down on a grill or under the broiler. Grill for 4 to 5 minutes. Turn zucchini over, brush with more oil, sprinkle with chile powder, oregano, and parmesan cheese and continue cooking 2 to 3 minutes. Zucchini should be slightly crisp when served.

JICAMA AND ORANGE SALAD

INGREDIENTS:

- 1/4 cup olive oil

- 1/4 cup wine vinegar

- 1 clove garlic

- 2 tbsp. lemon juice or 1 tbsp. lime juice

- 1/2 tsp. chile powder

- Dash of salt and pepper

- 6 oranges, peeled, sectioned, and seeded

- 1/4 lb. jicama, julienne

- 4 thin slices of red, sweet onion

DIRECTIONS:

Combine dressing ingredients in a jar and shake well. Refrigerate to let flavors blend. On salad plates, place a leaf of Romaine or head lettuce. Top with orange sections, onion slices, and jicama. Pour dressing over salad and serve immediately.

MACARONI AND CHEESE

INGREDIENTS:

- 1/2 pound bow tie pasta

- 1/2 cup cream

- 2 tbsp. butter

- 1/2 cup parmesan cheese

- 1/2 cup chopped green chile

DIRECTIONS:

Cook pasta al dente (8-10 min.). Drain. Heat cream and butter until butter is melted. Add parmesan cheese, green chile and heat until mixture just comes to a boil. Add pasta and toss to coat. Sprinkle with additional parmesan if desired and then top with Ass Kickin'™ Roasted Garlic Hot Sauce. Serves 4.

MEXICAN POTATO SALAD

INGREDIENTS:

• 6 potatoes boiled in skins

• 6 hard boiled eggs

• 1 medium onion, chopped

• 1 (4oz.) can diced chile

• 1 cup mayonnaise or salad dressing

• 1 to 2 tbsp. mustard - Ass Kickin'™ Mustard adds great flavor

• 2 tbsp. wine vinegar

• 1/4 cup milk

• Salt and pepper to taste

DIRECTIONS:

Peel and dice potatoes and eggs. Toss with onion and green chile in a large bowl. Combine mayonnaise, mustard, wine vinegar until well blended. Stir in milk, salt and pepper. Add dressing and gently stir to coat potato mixture. Refrigerate 2 to 3 hours to allow flavors to blend. Serves 6-8.

MEXICAN FRIED RICE

INGREDIENTS:

- 4 to 6 slices bacon, diced

- 1 cup long grain rice

- 2 cups beef or chicken bouillon

- 1 (16 oz.) can diced tomatoes

- 1 onion, chopped

- 1 or 2 tsp. oregano

- 1 tbsp. red pepper flakes or Ass Kickin'™ Hot Sauce
  to taste

DIRECTIONS:

Fry bacon until crisp. Remove bacon leaving 2 tbsp. of drippings in pan. Saute rice until lightly browned. Add onion, tomatoes, broth, oregano, and Ass Kickin'™ Hot Sauce. Simmer 25 to 30 minutes. Sprinkle crumbled bacon on top and serve. Serves 6-8.

PAPAS CON CHILE COLORADO

(potatoes with red chile)

INGREDIENTS:

• 2 large potatoes, thinly sliced

• 1 1/2 tbsp. oil (add some *heat* and use Ass Kickin'™ Olive Oil)

• 1 tbsp. ground chile powder

• 2 tbsp. flour

• 1 clove Ass Kickin'™ Garlic minced

• Salt to taste

• 2 1/2 cups water

DIRECTIONS:

Heat oil in skillet, add potatoes. Turn and stir potatoes as they are cooking until tender (a little more oil may be needed to keep potatoes from sticking). Remove potatoes from pan, add flour to remaining oil and brown slightly, adding chile, salt and garlic to flour and mixing well. Add water and bring to boil. Return potatoes to pan and stir to coat. Reduce heat and simmer for 10 minutes or until potatoes are tender.

PAPAS CON CHILE VERDE

(potatoes with green chile)

INGREDIENTS:

- 2 large potatoes, thinly sliced

- 1/2 onion, sliced

- 1 clove garlic minced or Ass Kickin'™ Garlic for a little heat

- 1 (4 oz.) can green chile, chopped

- 1 1/2 tbsp. oil

- Salt to taste

- 2 1/2 cups water

DIRECTIONS:

Heat oil in skillet, then hot add potatoes and brown for about 5 minutes, turning as necessary. Add onions and garlic and continue turning until onions are limp. Add green chile, salt, and water. Bring to the boil, reduce heat and cook 15 to 20 minutes or until potatoes are tender.

190

PASTA WITH CHILE AND SUN-DRIED TOMATOES

INGREDIENTS:

- 2 tbsp. crushed red chile

- 1/2 cup sun-dried tomatoes packed in oil, cut in slivers

- 1 cup Greek olives

- 1/2 cup fresh basil, loosely packed and chopped

- 1/2 cup fresh cilantro, loosely packed and chopped

- 3 cloves garlic minced

- 1/2 cup olive oil (extra virgin Ass Kickin'™ Olive Oil is wonderful in this recipe)

- 2 tbsp. oil from sun-dried tomatoes

- Salt and pepper to taste

- Parmesan cheese, grated

- 1 lb. penne pasta, cooked

DIRECTIONS:

Combine all ingredients except parmesan cheese and cooked pasta. Refrigerate 3 to 4 hours to blend flavors. Toss the pasta and cheese with the sauce and serve.

PAPAS CON CHILE

(POTATOES WITH CHILE)

INGREDIENTS:

- 4 potatoes, cubed
- 1 onion, chopped
- 1 (4 oz.) can chopped green chile
- 1 tbsp. parsley, minced
- Pinch of oregano, garlic salt and cumin
- 1 large tomato, peeled and diced
- 4 tbsp. bacon drippings or Ass Kickin'™ Olive Oil

DIRECTIONS:

Fry potatoes and onion over low heat in Ass Kickin'™ Olive Oil or bacon drippings. Add chile, tomato, and seasonings and stir until hot. Add a little hot water if needed.

RED CHILE PASTA

INGREDIENTS:

- 4 tbsp. ground red chile

- 4 tbsp. water

- 2 large eggs, at room temperature

- 2 tsp. olive oil - use Ass Kickin'™ Olive Oil to make it "*Red'* hot

- 2 cups flour

- Water as needed

DIRECTIONS:

Place red chile, water, eggs, and olive oil in food processor mixing until blended. Add flour and process until dough forms a ball. If dough remains crumbly, add water a teaspoon at a time until dough comes together. Remove from bowl and knead on floured board until dough is soft and elastic, about 5 minutes.

Work with 1/4 of the dough at a time, keeping the rest covered. Roll the dough using a pasta machine or a rolling pin into thin sheets. Cut pasta in strips. (If not using immediately, allow to dry overnight and store in air tight container.)

To cook fresh pasta, put in boiling water and cook several minutes until al dente. Cooking dried pasta requires more time, 7 to 10 minutes depending on thickness of pasta.

ROASTED GREEN CHILE POTATOES

INGREDIENTS:

• 4 tbsp. green chile or jalapeños, chopped

• 4 potatoes, thinly sliced

• 1 medium onion, quartered and sliced

• 2 cloves Ass Kickin'™ Garlic or fresh garlic chopped

• 1/4 cup parmesan cheese, grated

• 4 tbsp. butter or margarine

DIRECTIONS:

Prepare 4 double squares of aluminum foil. Spray each with vegetable oil and layer the potatoes, onions, garlic, and chile in the center of each square of foil. Sprinkle each packet with parmesan cheese, top with butter, salt and pepper. Wrap each packet loosely and seal.

Place packets on grill over medium hot coals and roast for 30 to 45 minutes turning occasionally so the potatoes cook evenly.

SCALLOPED POTATOES WITH CHILE

INGREDIENTS:

• 6 to 8 large potatoes, thinly sliced

• 1 medium onion, thinly sliced

• 1 (4 oz.) can green chiles, chopped

• 1 can cream of mushroom or cream of celery soup

• 1 cup milk

• 6 slices bacon, fried crisp and crumbled

• 8 oz. cheddar cheese, grated

• Ass Kickin'™ Roasted Garlic Hot Sauce

DIRECTIONS:

Grease 9 x 13" baking dish. Layer 1/2 of the potatoes, all of the onion, the cheese, and the rest of the potatoes in the dish. Mix together remaining ingredients and pour over top of potatoes. Cover dish with foil and bake in 375° oven for 1 1/2 to 2 hours or until potatoes are tender. Uncover last 10 minutes to brown. Serves 8. Add Ass Kickin'™ Roasted garlic to taste.

ASS KICKIN'™

STUFFED ZUCCHINI

INGREDIENTS:

- 4 small zucchini

- 1/4 cup onion, chopped

- 1 tbsp. butter or margarine, melted

- 2 eggs, slightly beaten

- 1 can whole kernel corn

- 1 (4 oz.) can green chiles, chopped

- 1/2 cup cracker crumbs

- 1/4 cup parmesan cheese

- 1/2 tsp. Ass Kickin'™ Popcorn Seasoning or salt to taste

- Dash each of garlic powder and oregano

DIRECTIONS:

Cut zucchini in half lengthwise and scoop out centers. Chop the pulp. Cook the onion in melted butter until tender. Combine the eggs, corn, chiles, cracker crumbs, cheese, chopped zucchini, and seasonings.

Sprinkle the zucchini shells with salt and spoon in the filling. Place in a baking dish and bake for 30 minutes. Sprinkle each squash with additional parmesan cheese. Serves 4.

VERDE ARROZ CASEROLA

(GREEN RICE CASSEROLE)

INGREDIENTS:

- 2 cups cooked rice

- 1 1/2 cup cheese, shredded

- 2 eggs, slightly beaten

- 1 onion, chopped

- 1 clove Ass Kickin'™ Garlic, chopped

- 2 tbsp. parsley, minced

- 1 (4oz.) can chopped green chile

- 1/4 tsp. oregano

- 1 small can whole kernel corn

- 1 small jar green olives

- 1 tbsp. Ass Kickin'™ Chicken Wing Sauce or chile sauce

- 1 cup beef broth

- Salt and pepper to taste

DIRECTIONS:

Heat oil over low heat and fry onion, garlic, green chiles, parsley, oregano, Ass Kickin'™ Chicken Wing Sauce or chile sauce, salt and pepper. Add beef broth and simmer gently for 5 minutes. In 3 quart casserole, combine rice, 1 cup of cheese, eggs, corn, olives and simmered sauce. Top with cheese. Bake 30 minutes in 350° oven.

ASS KICKIN'™ INDEX

Ass Kickin' Beverages

Ass Kickin' Bread, Tortillas & Pastries

Ass Kickin' Desserts

Ass Kickin' Eggs & Cheese

Ass Kickin' Side Dishes

Ass Kickin' Entrees

Ass Kickin' Sauces and Appetizers